"Hoover's straightforward, accessible appl
dents to craft their own writing processes b
interest them, being actively curious, and listening to others who
are also interested (as opposed merely to 'waiting to talk' themselves). Drawing on insights from Henry David Thoreau to Jean
Rhys to Joan Chittister to Steven Pinker to *The Office*, Hoover helps
equip students to resist mere noise generated in the age of social
media by engaging in academic writing as a living conversation that
can produce real change for good in the world. Complete with useful exercises and examples of how to put the method into practice,
the text makes a significant contribution to first-year composition
pedagogy."

—**Jill LeRoy-Frazier**, professor of cross-disciplinary studies,
East Tennessee State University

"Writing well requires certain kinds of human beings to do the
writing, and the kinds of human beings who write well only emerge
by writing well. Heather Hoover solves this Riddle of the Sphinx
not by forsaking writing but by teaching writing, and this book
without relent returns us, her readers, to reflect on the dynamic
nature and capacities and virtues of those human beings whom
we teach. We who teach writing, whether in college classrooms
or anywhere else human community happens, do well to heed."

—**Nathan P. Gilmour**, professor of English, Emmanuel College

"An absolute gem of a resource! It's not surprising that Hoover's
fresh reframing of composition as conversation transformed the
level of student engagement and investment in their writings. Applying the virtues of being curious, attentive, relatable, on topic,
engaging, open-minded, and generous to meaningful research,
in-class discussions, and academic writing inevitably transferred
into their daily lives. In an era where divisive discord dominates
the public arena and misinformation saturates the media, our
nation needs citizens embracing the critical and creative skills
this book encourages faculty to teach. The appendix also offers

excellent additional materials to reproduce. As a former university director of writing, I would have loved to have given this valuable resource to any adjunct faculty and teachers of writing preparing their classes! She's a wise sage!"

—**Linda Lawrence Hunt**, emerita director of Whitworth University's Writing Program; coauthor of *In the Long Run: A Study of Faculty in Three Writing-across-the-Curriculum Programs*

Composition
as
Conversation

Composition

as

Conversation

Seven Virtues
for Effective Writing

HEATHER M. HOOVER

Baker Academic

a division of Baker Publishing Group

Grand Rapids, Michigan

Published by Baker Academic
a division of Baker Publishing Group
www.bakeracademic.com

Printed in the United States of America

Library of Congress Cataloging-in-Publication Data
Names: Hoover, Heather M., author.
Title: Composition as conversation : seven virtues for effective writing / Heather M. Hoover.
Description: Grand Rapids : Baker Academic, a division of Baker Publishing Group, [2023] | Includes bibliographical references.
Identifiers: LCCN 2022059942 | ISBN 9781540966032 (paperback) | ISBN 9781540966506 (casebound) | ISBN 9781493441525 (ebook) | ISBN 9781493441532 (pdf)
Subjects: LCSH: English language—Rhetoric—Study and teaching (Higher) | LCGFT: Textbooks.
Classification: LCC PE1408 .H679 2023 | DDC 808/.042—dc23/eng/20221216
LC record available at https://lccn.loc.gov/2022059942

Baker Publishing Group publications use paper produced from sustainable forestry practices and post-consumer waste whenever possible.

23   24   25   26   27   28   29   7   6   5   4   3   2   1

For all my students

Contents

Acknowledgments

Fifteen years (at least) of conversations have helped shape me and the composition program at the university where I teach. I am grateful and lucky to partner in conversation with some very generous and wise people.

Thanks to Alan Holmes from East Tennessee State University for sifting through ideas with me as a grad student, one of my first pedagogical models of how generous listening can motivate engaged writing.

I am lucky to work with many generous administrators who have helped prioritize writing for students. Particular thanks to Mark Matson, my first academic dean, for dreaming big with me about interdisciplinary composition and for supporting my curricular vision. Thanks to registrar Stacy Dahlman for making our composition conference possible during finals week, and to Joy Drinnon, director of undergraduate research, for her continued support and sponsorship of our conference.

I owe a great debt to my colleagues (who are also my friends) for encouraging and facilitating this book: Miriam Perkins, who convinced me to take a sabbatical, and who always offers wise counsel and generous support; Phil Kenneson, who shepherded my sabbatical proposal; Craig Farmer, who shared his own writing journey with me; Todd Edmondson, Tim Dillon, and Michael

Blouin, who taught extra courses in my stead and encouraged me at every turn; Amy Edmonds, Kayla Walker Edin, and Shauna Nefos Webb, whose friendship, generous conversation, and support are gifts beyond measure; Grete Scott, for her wit, friendship, and invaluable composition collaboration; Mary Jackson, whose library expertise helps make research conversations possible (and painless); David Kiger, who made a quiet working space for me in the seminary library; Daniel Silliman, who gave graciously of his time and talent; Amy Linnemann, whose own love of words inspired and encouraged me from afar; and J. P. Abner, who reminded me how unique the composition classroom can be as we walked together between classes.

I would also like to thank my wonderful team at Baker Academic. Thanks for answering all my questions with generosity and patience. Special thanks to Dave Nelson for believing in this project, to Anna Gissing for her careful editing, and to Eric Salo and the copyediting team who stayed in conversation with me.

My students give me great hope for the future, and it is my privilege to be in conversation with them. Special thanks to Norma Rendon, Holly Lay, Drake Shull, Casey Williams, Seth Nicol, Amy Shumaker, Evan Magness, Reece Anderson, and Bethany Hicks, whose stories or work appear in some form in this book. Special thanks to Danielle Littleton, whose sophomore research on citation styles nearly a decade ago and impeccable memory today led me to Anthony Grafton's work.

Finally, I am grateful to have three inspiring and gracious conversational partners who sharpen and improve me every day living right in my house. Randy, Owen, and Violet, you model how to stay in conversation even when it is difficult, how to agree and disagree lovingly, how to reconsider a position with care, and how to ask the very best questions. I am glad to be in conversation with you always.

Introduction

Composition as Conversation: Engaging in Meaningful Academic Dialogue

The composition classroom is much more than word counts and gallons of spilled red ink, and yet even the most enthusiastic writing instructor may have difficulty fostering a love of academic writing in students. Too often, students view composition requirements in high school or at the undergraduate level as a check mark, something to be endured rather than a vital part of their education. That the requirement remains in so many institutions speaks to its importance, though perhaps its very nature as a requirement also generates resistance (and sometimes dread). Students come to my writing classes at a private liberal arts college in varying states of that resistance and dread. Some come excited and ready to add to their writing training, some come believing that a writing course is not necessary for their chosen career, and some come with no writing experience at all. Few students come expecting that their first-year or second-year essays will matter much to them or to me. I have been teaching writing at some level for almost twenty-five years, and if student writing did not matter to me that would mean the better part of my life has been wasted. I have as much at stake in the writing classroom as do my students.

Early in my teaching career, a student resolutely declared that she was "rubbish at essays" but that didn't matter because she was a *creative* writer. Of course, the art of communication is not so different in either genre, but because she did not see academic writing as a creative space, she dismissed it out of hand. She *did* write lovely short stories, and she was working on a novel in which she developed characters with depth and nuance. Yet in her academic writing she could not sustain a paragraph, and evidence was strewn throughout her paper like research confetti. Despite class exercises and mini-lessons and lectures on craft, she did not see academic writing's potential to communicate her voice. I knew in that moment that I had to make a better connection between writing and clear communication for my students. I needed to help students better invest in their academic writing voices.

When I was a little girl learning to tie my shoes, a well-meaning adult, someone who had tied thousands of shoelaces, told me to "make a loop, bring it around and through, and like *magic*" my shoes would be tied. Try as I might, the magic never happened, leaving me feeling frustrated and incompetent. It turns out that I was missing quite a few small but necessary motions for those shoes to stay on my feet. In fact, because I was so focused on the process of tying my shoes, I missed the actual *purpose* of my actions. I was so busy trying to follow the formula that I distanced myself from the goal, unwittingly making the task harder for myself. For students and instructors, sometimes the composition classroom feels a bit like that interaction: we focus so intently on breaking writing into a process that it loses its dynamic purpose and students lose sight of themselves in their writing. Of course, the key to good writing is not in waiting for magic, but in practicing the kind of thinking and engagement that will help us have something meaningful to say. And just like tying shoes, writing has more than one path to that kind of effective communication.

This book is designed to help students and instructors demystify writing by framing it as an ethical and effective conversation, one that fosters good listening and thoughtful response focused on the virtues of dialogue rather than rigid, systematic process. Framing academic writing as a conversation encourages students to think of their audience, the evidence, the opposition, the past, the contemporary moment, and even themselves as worthy and essential conversational partners. On the first day of each new semester, I ask students to make a list describing the best conversationalists they know. In the Fall 2019 semester, their answers included *curious, attentive, relatable, on topic, engaging, open-minded,* and *generous*. These attributes, generated in conversation with my students, frame my exploration of the composition-as-conversation classroom.

When we think about writing as a conversation, it changes the way we think about the pieces and parts of an essay. What writing teacher has not read a student introduction that begins with a random quotation, a banal dictionary definition, or some variation of "throughout history"? But students *know* how to introduce themselves in many different contexts. Not one of them would, upon meeting a new person, state a definition of male or female or student or soccer player. Neither would students introduce themselves by sharing the story of their birth or quoting Einstein. Instead, they would assess the situation and offer the most relevant information to help us know them in that moment and context. The conversational frame has transformed my classroom over the past decade. Simply changing my approach to teaching the subject has helped students generate some of the most meaningful work I have seen from student writers. My students invest more deeply in their work, often choosing to continue their research in upper-division studies. They talk to one another about their research in and out of the classroom. They spend time with the research librarian and their academic advisors thinking about their topics. They learn that a conversation is more vibrant when it includes more voices, but they also learn that it requires more patience, and often more listening.

One assignment midway between rough and final drafts asks students to extend the conversation about their topics beyond campus and into the community. These conversations help students think about research applications from practical and lived perspectives. Extending the dialogue beyond the classroom helps students see realistic applications of their work, and it helps them revise and reframe more compassionately. Our semester culminates in an academic conference where we emphasize the importance of the dynamic discourse that becomes possible when participants invest in their own and one another's work. The thirty minutes of discussion following the panel presentations are some of the finest discussions I have ever witnessed at an academic conference.

From idea generation to the final works cited page, academic writing should cultivate lively discussion and promote critical and creative thinking. Especially at the high school and early undergraduate levels, writing needs to be inclusive, generous, and carefully researched. In this contemporary moment when students have access to so many opinions and data, they need tools to help them participate thoughtfully and responsibly in a conversation where their voices should and do matter. That kind of classroom might indeed feel enchanting, in part because we have become accustomed to more vitriolic discourse; yet civil conversation is not only accessible to everyone but also essential to the health of our communities and the larger civic body. Throughout this book, I draw on the insights and wisdom of philosophers, religious mystics, poets, and novelists, as well as many other types of scholars who have inspired my teaching and writing. Being in conversation with these thinkers, as well as with my students and colleagues, helps me to be a better teacher, writer, and human being.

I use the seven conversational virtues my students offered to explore writing's potential to transform. Of course, writing is still a process, but it does not have to be a rigid, exclusive process. Like the best of conversations, academic writing has the potential to surprise and delight. Though I include some assignment templates and examples, this book is not intended to be prescriptive. Instead, I hope what you will find here is my love letter to the writing class-room's potential to transform us. In the spirit of conversation, I hope that you develop your own response to these ideas, finding ways to apply and implement dialogue in your own writing work.

one

Be Curious

When we are young, we can fire hundreds of questions an hour at our parents. Why do my eyes blink? How many leaves are on that tree? How much does a cloud weigh? Why do I need to sleep? Curiosity fuels these questions, along with our emerging self-awareness and desire to connect to the world around us. When my own children were small, their questions (even when they seemed naive) helped *me* think about the world in new ways. But more importantly, these questions brought us into new and deeper relationship. Their curiosity paved the way for interesting and stimulating conversations. (Thanks to my son's questions, I now know how much a cloud weighs, and it is surprisingly heavy.) Our early questions reflect a burgeoning, uninhibited curiosity, something writer Elizabeth Gilbert believes can serve us well for our entire lives. Gilbert observes from her own experience that curiosity is always at our disposal, but passion may strike suddenly and hot.[1] In her book *Big Magic*, she makes the case for living a life not of passion-fueled interests and clarion calling but of quiet, "turn

1. Gilbert, *Big Magic*, 238.

your head a quarter of an inch" curiosity.[2] As we grow, many of us learn to tame our persistent questions, and many students learn to separate their own interests from their academic work. The writing classroom can reenergize our curiosity, helping us not only to turn our heads but to level our gaze at what interests us. In the writing classroom, we practice refining our questions to develop and broaden our interests as well as the discussion.

Writing instructors may find it easier or expedient to assign topics, though doing so often robs students of their autonomy and excitement for a writing project. Still, some writers balk at the freedom to choose. Each semester, I encounter several students who complain that they don't know what to write about. When I push them to write about something that interests them, those students often struggle to find much beyond their daily routine. In those cases, I wish I could send them away for a few weeks with no tasks but to observe and listen—to rekindle the curious fire of their early selves, turning their heads toward whatever catches their attention. Alas, the pace of a school calendar does not permit that luxury. Taking some time in the classroom to model this process, then, is often helpful and necessary. My first question to writers struggling with topic choice is simply "What interests you?" Whatever the answer, the next question is "What questions do you have about that topic?" Sometimes writers wait for a lightning bolt of inspiration when the possibilities for inquiry are much closer at hand. Though I do not assign topics in my writing classroom, students will inevitably encounter an assigned topic at some point, and knowing how to connect what interests them with an assigned topic can invigorate their writing. For example, I study literature, but one of my main interests is food and cooking. A required essay on nineteenth-century class distinction in a Dickens novel might offer an opportunity to question how meals reveal character

2. Krista Tippett, "Elizabeth Gilbert: Choosing Curiosity over Fear," *On Being with Krista Tippett* (podcast), July 7, 2016, https://onbeing.org/programs/elizabeth -gilbert-choosing-curiosity-over-fear-may2018.

relationships or status. Writers who develop their curiosity can find entries into nearly any topic or conversation.

Most writers *do* know how to have meaningful personal conversations by asking good questions, but they need help bringing that skill onto the page. It takes practice to look closely at situations and texts and ask effective questions. Even our daily conversations require effort to rise above the level of information exchange. Consider the kinds of perfunctory questions we ask one another daily:

Did you sleep well?
How was your day?
How are you?
What does your schedule look like?
Where do you want to eat?

These types of questions masquerade as open-ended and curious, but they rarely drive dynamic interchange. Often, only in the intimacy of family or long friendship can these questions be productive, but even in familiarity such questions often falter, especially if we stop there. In my family, we still need to work to pay attention to one another and ask better questions that will develop meaningful conversation. It is easy to feel like we are talking, only to realize later that very little was actually said. Consider the difference between these two pairs of questions:

How was your day? and What was something funny that happened today?

What did you do today in English? and What character resonated with you in your reading today?

The differences in these two approaches are perspective and particularity. If I want deeper conversation with my teenage son, I need to ask a better question. I need to observe how he spends his time. I need to think about his day as he experiences it and, of course, I need to be specific so that he can bring focus to his reply. This kind of question-asking requires me to participate in the asking as much as the answering. One of the best conversationalists I know is a young woman named Amy who asks unpredictable and interesting questions. On the long ride to New York City for a course trip, her questions took some of the other students by surprise. To their credit, they put down their devices and engaged with her, and what followed was a true exchange of ideas, not simply information. As it happens, Amy is also one of the most curious people I have ever met, not only about ideas but about those around her. When her fellow travelers responded to her probing questions, she listened carefully, each response providing an opportunity to pursue a new direction. As Marilyn Chandler McEntyre observes, curiosity not only sparks conversations but also sustains them.[3] She writes that "conversation pursued in this spirit is full of surprise. It connects one idea or thought or analogy with another in ways that could not have been predicted."[4] Perhaps it is unsurprising that after several hours of driving together across the country, we were all exhausted from the depth and vigor of the discussion.

Beginning a conversation requires humility, risk, and commitment. Too often, the writing conversation is predictable. Writers receive a topic, they craft a thesis, and they find evidence to support their ideas. The predictable five-paragraph structure dictates the flow of the writing, and long-held practices dictate their approach to the topic. The process itself, as it has been distilled over time and throughout their years of learning, leaves little room for surprise. Writers approach topics with perfunctory "How are you today?" questions, and instead of a dynamic conversation, the result is often simply a recital of information. In his talks on conversation, Theodore Zeldin lauds "the kind of conversation . . . in which you start with a willingness to emerge a slightly different person."[5]

3. McEntyre, *Caring for Words in a Culture of Lies*, 99–101.
4. McEntyre, *Caring for Words in a Culture of Lies*, 101.
5. Zeldin, *Conversation*, 3.

Conversation that changes the world will likely change us first. Ultimately, asking meaningful questions brings writers into the lives of their community, be it scholarly or otherwise.

How to Have Ideas: Notice, Engage, Make Meaning

Of course, not every writer lands in a writing class with Amy's proclivity for conversation. For the first few class periods, then, we focus on having ideas. In the classroom, as in life, we cannot simply jump into a conversation unprepared. Topic development is a crucial step in the writing process, and I prioritize it for students. We begin by scanning headlines in various news magazines and websites. I introduce them to *Smithsonian* magazine or *JSTOR Daily* for examples of writing spurred by genuine curiosity. We are not searching these headlines for topic ideas, but for inspiration. Often, the time we spend sifting through these sources triggers a response, a reminder of something the students are genuinely curious about.

After we spend some time reading inspiring articles, we choose one to consider carefully together as a class. We note the title—is that what drew us in? We talk about the tone, the evidence, the structure, the introduction—all these components of the piece giving us a sense of how to generate and sustain interest in a subject—and *then* we respond. I ask writers to draft a list of questions they would ask the author or would like to pursue on their own. This process brings writers into a conversation, reminding them that their role as readers is not to consume information passively, but to engage intentionally.

After this time in class, I send students "into the wild" to observe on their own. Some fruitful observation activities include:

- reading the lyrics of a favorite song multiple times, making note of dominant images or diction
- watching a favorite movie again, this time asking questions as a participant rather than simply passively consuming entertainment

- reading a single passage from a book multiple times, making note of particularities and the potential connection to the rest of the story
- taking a walk with a journal in hand for writing down observations
- watching a sports event looking for patterns or influences on the play
- considering a daily process in detail, such as the cafeteria experience or traffic patterns in town

These kinds of activities help writers begin to see the potential for good questions everywhere. Of course, this process is related to close reading, but it should (and does) apply to all manner of "texts," written or not. One writer told me that I had "broken" her, because she now sees the potential to ask questions about everything. I could have shown her the ever-growing list of topics I want to write about that I keep tacked to my office bulletin board in response. Curiosity, it turns out, can become a rewarding and persistent habit.

After some practice asking questions, we spend time together observing a short text, perhaps a movie poster or poem, before writers choose their own for individual work. In order to model observational skills from the same vantage point as writers new to a topic, I select a text new to me as well. If I bring in a text I have researched extensively, it can be daunting to writers encountering that text for the first time. My familiarity with a piece can inhibit their flow of ideas. Instead, we practice being curious together, framing questions, and comparing observations of this new text. Though the exercise inevitably elicits some similar observations, each group develops unique ideas connected to their own contexts and perspectives. The text becomes not a fixed artifact but rather the site of dynamic investigation. Like our conversations in the van on our way to New York, the work is both rewarding and exhausting.

One semester, I noticed a bulletin board in one of the education classrooms bedecked in school colors and a collection of promotional images. The board, perhaps part of an assignment for education students, presented a perfect collective entry to analysis. In class, I asked the writers to spend five minutes writing down everything they noticed about the arrangement, the colors, the content, and the images. Then I asked them to spend five more minutes writing down everything they thought might be missing from the board's representation. I compiled all their observations on a whiteboard. After this time spent observing, I asked them to consider what they thought the purpose of the board might be. Some suggested it was an exercise in bulletin board design, while others suggested it might be intended to attract students to the school. These observations led one student to ask, "If the students are already in a classroom, why would they need to be enticed to apply?" Another asked, "What message does this combination of materials suggest about the school?" Even if the bulletin board was simply an exercise, they argued, its composition made a statement about the school's ethos.

Throughout this process, students became increasingly more engaged with a bulletin board that most of us would have paid little attention to otherwise. Students observed that the board featured athletics, but that the arts and academics were underrepresented. Some students cynically commented that the school only cares about athletics. But some of the athletes objected, asserting that academics matter to all students. Their observations led to important questions and discussion in which students had to listen to one another and be willing to put aside their assumptions. The questions shifted from "Why doesn't the school care about academics and the arts?" to "What might be influencing the way this board represents the school's ethos?" The second of those questions generated far more interesting (and supportable) conversation. We began to consider all the possibilities: marketing priorities that motivate promotional choices, changing student demographics, and the influence of school spirit. By the end of the class period, we had engaged deeply with this visual text and our observations had generated meaningful conversation. We had also learned that we would need more information and a variety of perspectives if we wanted to make substantive claims about the board. It is too easy to make assumptions and dismiss the opportunity for this kind of intellectual work.

Before writers begin their own work in earnest, we practice with several samples. We consider together a movie poster, a short story, a micro-short story, a situation (such as a current trend), and a few lines from a work of fiction. With each one, we follow the same process: we engage deeply by reading or spending time with the text, spend time observing what is there and not there, and develop a list of questions. After several class periods of modeling and discussion, writers are ready to bring in their own potential topics and begin annotations and explications of their own.

Annotations trace our engagement with texts. Most of us have experience underlining or highlighting meaningful words and passages, and thus the general task is not new to most writers. But not all annotations are helpful, and guiding writers through the process is important. We often take a short poem or editorial and work through it together in class, as we did with the bulletin board. We focus on what is there, what is not there, and structure. We look for important words and repetitions, syntax, omissions, blind spots, juxtapositions, and the architecture of the argument. Not all of these observations will be important to the eventual analysis, but intentional engagement with the text will serve writers well. Writers who have "no idea what to say" about a text often have few or unhelpful annotations. Before they are allowed to change topics, I ask them to spend more time with the text, using our corporate model as a guide. Asking different questions of a text can result in a different, often more fruitful and interesting conversation.

Annotation prepares students for a short explication assignment. Explication is an interpretive activity that is often a first step toward analysis, useful because it helps kindle and develop observations.

To "explicate" a text means to "unfold" it by looking closely at its details and construction. Explicating encourages immersion in the text, the active listening that I will take up in the next chapter. In a practical sense, it demonstrates to students that they *can* have ideas in response to a text, because it does not require secondary resources. Instead, the explication process requires students to engage the subject intentionally and repeatedly. Each time they return to the text, they build on their previous experience. The motivating first question "What does this mean?" gives way to more focused responses that facilitate a deeper and more productive conversation with the text. Explications also encourage a more intimate and specific dialogue with the text. It is impossible in just two or three pages to focus on all the details of a text, and students are often astounded that they have so much to say about a short passage, a few minutes of a movie, or even an absence in a photo or painting.

After the annotation and explication process, we spend some time in the library. Armed with substantive observations about their topic or text, writers follow leads, check out new directions and ideas, and begin charting a potential course through their ideas. At this point, the writers have no thesis, no obligation, just some ideas that more research helps them define and clarify. Sometimes writers find that someone else has already had their idea and has published work on their exact topic. Though I encourage students in this first essay project to choose topics that are less well known, it is an important skill to be able to add to a conversation. If the writer discovers that broad scholarship on the topic already exists, we work together to consider a response that might extend or broaden the discussion. Finding that another researcher has investigated the same path can be disappointing, as if a research door has closed, but it also offers an exciting opportunity to continue a research conversation by changing the context or adding a component. Disagreement and rebuttal can develop new and interesting pathways for conversation. Even fiction writers springboard from other writers' work, like the great Jean Rhys, whose

Wide Sargasso Sea deepens and refutes Charlotte Brontë's portrait of "the madwoman in the attic" from *Jane Eyre*. Not being the first to a topic does not mean we cannot contribute to the conversation.

If a topic is particularly contemporary, regional, or specific, writers may not find any peer-reviewed information at all in journals or databases. In that case, we work on what we call "parallel research." Clearly, no peer-reviewed research would have been available about our bulletin board topic, but pursuing that idea could easily involve research about private colleges, changing student demographics, the increase in niche athletics, or school marketing campaigns. Writers might also find strong primary research in the school's data or on its website.

Writing about texts, whether traditional written texts or atypical texts such as movies or museum exhibits or photos, offers a concrete entry point to the research dialogue. Writers work with an artifact that has a clear message; they listen and engage with that message and respond. Though the early writing project in my writing classroom makes room for atypical, non-written texts, it is still focused fundamentally on creative works. As an entry point, responding to a creative text can help hone research and questioning skills, yet even at my small liberal arts school, most students major in a vocational subject such as engineering or nursing. Engaging with a text through critical analysis and dialogue certainly transfers as a skill, but students still need a chance to practice applying that skill to their field of study or interest, a chance to generate ideas that might be meaningful to them and to their academic communities. After writers practice working with texts, then, they work on applying those newly polished skills of annotation and question-development to a more comprehensive research project.

Academic Alchemy

Most instructors have had the opportunity to attend an academic conference at which like-minded and curious scholars gather to share research and innovation. Coming together around a topic generates enthusiasm, purpose, excitement, and what I like to call "academic alchemy." This ordinary-turned-extraordinary transformation happens in my classroom frequently when people who have immersed themselves in the same material come together for discussion that generates new ideas and insights that could only happen in a moment of collaboration. This type of "alchemy" often occurs under "directed freedom," in which the instructor selects a theme or a passage, but students have the freedom to associate, apply, and interpret, to follow the intellectual paths wherever they might lead. Academic conferences are similar in that they often coalesce around a theme, dividing groups of ideas into "panels" of thinkers offering different perspectives on subthemes of the conference. In the writing classroom, it is similarly helpful to offer students a theme, some sort of big idea to help focus and stimulate their thinking.

In our composition program, we host an actual conference at the end of the semester for all students (more on the conference in chap. 7). Together, my colleagues and I craft a germane call for papers (CFP) that has some cultural relevance (see appendix 1). To model the distillation from thematic idea to potential research topic, each instructor drafts and submits a sample research problem and question on a topic that the instructor finds meaningful. (Engaging in this process as a team provides a unique conversation opportunity for me and my colleagues. We teach this material each fall, but this pre-semester conversation invigorates us and helps us connect with the work we ask of our incoming writers.) In 2022, we hosted our tenth writing conference, having covered themes such as ethics and trust, sustainability, intersectionality, reconciliation, and imagination. Whatever the topic, a theme offers the directed freedom so conducive to stimulating thinking.

Once writers have become familiar with the CFP, we work together in class to begin organizing ideas into potential research topics. Writers notice immediately the research and reading integral to the sample research questions. The sample research problems and questions demonstrate the importance of preliminary research in articulating ideas clearly while emphasizing the curiosity and careful consideration required to enter the research conversation. Once we have reflected on the sample research questions, we brainstorm responses to the CFP. Listing each student's major on the board, I ask the class to generate obvious entries to the theme. For example, a biology major's obvious entry to the theme of sustainability might be climate change. I then ask the entire class to respond with one more specific or local application of the obvious entry to the theme and one wacky, not-so-obvious one. In one of these sessions, a biology major immediately narrowed the theme to his own backyard, quite literally, by thinking about an infestation of starlings in his neighborhood, while the rest of the class, few of whom majored in biology, asked about the sustainability of intense pre-med preparation for athletic scholarship students. The same thematic call stimulated two completely different but worthwhile topics.

Notably, this process takes several class periods, followed by at least one class session for research in the library before writers craft a formal proposal. All the while, I am having conversations with students and facilitating conversations between students about their ideas, asking them why they want to pursue this topic, what makes them want to spend the next twelve weeks doing this research, and what they think or hope they can contribute to the conversation. In some of the most powerful conversations I have had during this interlude, students confess that they do not really want to write about the topic at all, that they are pursuing it because it seems "academic." One young woman named Norma, responding to a CFP on interdependence and ecosystems, came to me proposing she write about "development of feminism in Mexico and in the United States." She had a sort of vague idea about what that meant—the interchange of beliefs and influences—but she did not seem terribly enthusiastic about it. I asked her, "What makes you want to write about feminism?" Her answer was far more specific and compelling than "feminism," ranging from her own education and upbringing to machismo and gender roles in her own family. She did not really want to write about feminism as a movement or critical lens, but the term felt more academic than her true interest. The freedom to explore what truly mattered to her generated a much more engaging inquiry. Her subsequent research proposal focused on how evolving systems of religion and family (by way of immigration and interconnection) were changing the traditional machismo expectation for Mexican men. Though feminism was there in her research, her actual focus meant far more to her, to me, and to her community than a paper on feminism writ large.

My conversation with Norma simply helped her reframe her understanding of research writing. Many students equate academic research with the arcane and abstract—and to be fair, some academic research is just that. But the best research retains that spark of personal curiosity. Transcendentalist writer and naturalist Henry David Thoreau claimed that "the purest science is still biographical."[6] To the transcendental mind, science and research could not be considered separately from the people conducting the experiments, despite the objectivity and rigor in the approach and method. The narrator of Yaa Gyasi's 2020 novel *Transcendent Kingdom* is a scientist who realizes that though her lab results must be factual and stripped of self, her research ultimately is an extension of who she is.[7] Gyasi's novel reminds us that even the most objective science can be motivated by intensely personal interest, heartbreak, or affection. So many students see research as, at best, a monologue, or at worst, a dictation destined for the dead end of their instructor's desk. Helping students understand that their own interests can and should shape the conversation helps them to engage more enthusiastically and authentically with their research work.

6. Thoreau, *Week on the Concord*, 295.
7. Gyasi, *Transcendent Kingdom*, 251–52.

Entering the Conversation

Finally, after several weeks of preparation and research, writers are ready to draft and submit a research proposal, the formal
entry into the conversation. Over the years, I have developed a
template (appendix 2) for the research proposal that emphasizes
first the writer's voice and motivation, then the writer's questions
contextualized by the broader conversation, and finally, a research
strategy. Grounding the proposal in a writer's own convictions or
personal story establishes a bond, a commitment to the "back and
forth" of conversation. Some writers realize for the first time that
their personal stories and experiences can and do motivate good
research. Later, we will use the first section of the research proposal to help assess our biases and blind spots, but we might also
use it to connect with an audience who needs to see why the topic
matters to the writer before they invest in it themselves. Research
proposals promote a deliberate approach to meaningful conversation, all the while demonstrating to students that they do indeed
have something to say. The proposals allow me to engage with my
writers long before they submit a rough draft or even a thesis, and
to nudge them in productive and helpful directions.

The research proposal marshals a writer's initial curiosity and
provides a starting point for upcoming research. For weeks, writers
have observed, asked questions, refined questions, and listened to
research and to their peers. Even with all that work, sometimes
the proposal looks nothing like the finished project, in part because writers who enter the conversation willing to emerge, as
Zeldin observes, "a slightly different person" find that the process
is fluid and dynamic. Conversation begins with an invitation to
consider the world from a different perspective. The philosopher
Michel Foucault says curiosity "evokes the care one takes of what
exists and what might exist . . . a readiness to find what surrounds
us strange and odd; a certain determination to throw off familiar ways of thought and to look at the same things in a different

way."[8] Care for one another, for "what exists and what might exist," sets aside fear in favor of discovery. When we invest in our community and the world around us, we ask interested and interesting questions, the kind that require attention and effort. And when we invest in asking effective questions, we are more prepared to listen to the answers, to participate in the dialogue, and to risk being changed ourselves. Curiosity can be as simple as asking "What interests me?" and listening for the response, harking back to our toddler selves who wanted to know more about everything from clouds to the science of sleep. The writing classroom facilitates essential inquisitive space where simply being curious evokes the care needed for thought-provoking and meaningful conversations.

8. Foucault, *Politics, Philosophy, Culture*, 328.

two

Be Attentive

In a deleted scene of the 1994 Quentin Tarantino movie *Pulp Fiction*, Mia Wallace asks Vincent Vega, "In conversation, do you listen or wait to talk?" He considers her question and responds truthfully: "I have to admit that I wait to talk, but I'm trying harder to listen."[1] Perhaps we are all guilty of "waiting to talk" at some point in our conversational lives, or worse, we may not even wait, but forge ahead with our own arguments or agendas, cutting off the voices around us. Listening well means exercising a kind of restraint that invites rumination and makes space for new ideas to flourish.

Research conversations require a similar humility and patience. Too often, students dive into drafting without taking time to listen well. Every semester I ask students how they approach research and incorporating evidence into their writing, and every semester, many more students than I would hope characterize research as a necessary evil. Some writers even consider research something to be added at the end, *after* they are finished writing! In

1. *Pulp Fiction*, directed by Quentin Tarantino (1994; Burbank, CA: Walt Disney Studios, 1998), DVD.

a well-intentioned effort to teach the mechanics of research and integration, some instructors introduce early writing students to research as citation-per-paragraph quotas rather than as part of a meaningful dialogue, inadvertently undermining the depth of a research conversation. Instructors who expect students to have something to say before they have engaged in careful listening impoverish writers' experience with researching and writing. For many reasons, then, writers often come to the page unprepared to talk but doing it anyway.

Benedictine nun and theologian Joan Chittister reflects on the Rule of Benedict, which begins with a call to listen as a "plan" or "guidepost" that bends life in a particular direction, a way of engaging with life.[2] As a plan for engaging with life, listening is both simple and complex. She explains that in the Benedictine order, intentional listening is regarded as the beginning of spiritual wisdom, of full immersion in the lives of others, of deep engagement with the Scriptures, and of a humble posture toward creation. A similar observation could be made about the writing conversation, and for many of the same reasons. Before we can have something to say, Chittister writes, we must pay attention and be willing "to change ourselves and the world."[3] She echoes Theodore Zeldin and many others who have come to understand conversation as a deeply transformative endeavor that requires careful, intentional attention.

It may be difficult to see how a few words spoken or a few paragraphs written could change us or the world, especially because, as Chittister observes, "we prefer to hear ourselves" rather than be "called beyond ourselves."[4] Listening is risky, because it almost always requires empathy; it is first and foremost an act of selflessness that calls others into dialogue with us. Those few words spoken or paragraphs written, developed through a discipline of listening

2. Chittister, *Wisdom Distilled from the Daily*, 7.
3. Chittister, *Wisdom Distilled from the Daily*, 19.
4. Chittister, *Wisdom Distilled from the Daily*, 15.

to wise counsel and the perspectives and experiences of others, can only change the world if they first change us. And we must be *willing* to be changed. Zeldin observes that "humans have already changed the world several times by changing the way they have conversations."[5] He cites the Enlightenment, the Renaissance, the civil rights movement, and the women's rights movement among examples of moments when listening differently changed the course of history. Today, we are beginning to listen to our planet and change the way we have conversations about climate. One of my favorite contemporary climate scientists, Katharine Hayhoe, believes that the only way to make inroads toward positive climate action is to change the conversation by listening. She writes that once you have asked a question, "the most important thing to do is to listen and then keep listening . . . because the longer you listen, the more you'll understand."[6] Hayhoe has decades of experience and piles of data that would help her make her case hundreds of times over, yet she still prioritizes listening to those who might disagree with her so that she can frame a more effective, empathetic response.

Ethical Research Practices

Ethical research practices may seem more important for scientists or medical research, and indeed, these fields have clear ethical principles of research, such as informed consent, social and scientific validity, and independent review. But for high school students or undergraduates who are beginning writers, what does it mean to maintain ethical research practices? Like Hayhoe, we need to listen to a combination and variety of sources that provide objective and subjective experiences if we are going to respond with wisdom and empathy. A few years ago, a vibrant and witty young man stayed after class each day, eager to debate current events. Influenced

5. Zeldin, *Conversation*, 7.
6. Hayhoe, *Saving Us*, 236.

by the combative conversational style of news networks, he was eager to spar with me. When I asked him about his sources, he could only name one. I invited him to sample several other news outlets and some primary source data, promising him that once he did, we would talk. Over the next few semesters, he *did* seek out a variety of sources. On some points, he changed his thinking, while on others, he expanded his depth of knowledge. Instead of making him more combative, though, that new depth of knowledge encouraged even more listening on his part. My goal was not for him to change his thinking, of course, but for him to know why he believed what he believed, and for him to enter each conversation willing to consider deeply another point of view. Each semester, I introduce students to a media bias chart and ask them to read something from both ends of the spectrum and something from in between. We often look up one particular subject in multiple outlets to assess how different biases color the presentation as well as our reception. I have the good fortune of working with an enthusiastic and creative research librarian who visits my classes each semester to introduce students to databases and search engines. She helps students refine their searches and understand the algorithms behind them. Though many writers are "digital natives," they often need training to move beyond a Google search. Knowing where and how to search gives us access to more voices. Ethical research practices are rooted in the same attention to empathy and diversity that drives meaningful conversation, and similarly, these skills require good models and opportunities for practice.

Multiple points of view. Diversifying the conversation, as my student did by seeking out multiple points of view, is one step toward an ethical research practice. Anyone born after 2000 has grown up with nearly instantaneous access to all kinds of information, but all that access does not always translate to discernment or variety. Personal proclivities and partiality drive newsfeed algorithms to ensure we remain absorbed. The great essayist Michel de Montaigne *wanted* people to argue with him, because he found agreement "boring and intellectually deadening."[7] Though many networks still feature representatives of opposite sides shouting at one another, I'm afraid he would find most of today's content less than stimulating. Montaigne desired well-considered debate with the potential for change, not emotional arguments intended to debase the opposition. Exercises such as the annotated bibliography and the counterargument summary (which I will take up later in this chapter) help writers come to a table set with many diverse dishes rather than iterations of the same dish.

Use valid material. The second ethical research principle is to use valid material. I ask my students to review journal articles and books to practice evaluating source content. Finding a source in a database or in an academic journal does not guarantee its validity, and what might have been perfectly acceptable or valid thirty years ago might not hold for a contemporary argument. Sometimes verifying the validity of a source requires even more research: learning about the career and contributions of the author, understanding the context of the research, determining who funded the survey, or tracking down references from the bibliography. To begin a single conversation, it sometimes seems, is to begin a thousand conversations.

I like to share with my students two sources that treat Robert Frost's well-known poem "Stopping by Woods on a Snowy Evening." One source cites Frost's imagery and the geography of New England to claim the poem's existential nature, and extends that argument to claim that a New England ethos would motivate the speaker to carry on despite hardship.[8] The other source claims, by virtue of the time of year and some bells, that the speaker is Santa Claus.[9] Both sources were published in reputable journals, one in the mid-twentieth century and one much more recently. Though each author cites evidence and carefully outlines an argument, students often find both arguments to be incomplete, in part because those

---

7. Miller, *Conversation*, 1.
8. Monteiro, "Suicide and the New England Conscience," 145–51.
9. Coursen, "Ghost of Christmas Past," 236–38.

arguments themselves present such abridged conversations with the poem and the scholarship surrounding it. Spending time with the bibliographies and with the poem itself yields an interesting discussion about how we might evaluate each source for use in our own work. Through this exercise, we learn to consider even published articles carefully, to engage in a dialogue with a source rather than simply cherry-picking a few nice quotations, and to build our own claims in conversation with source material.

Careful representation and citation. A third ethical research principle is honesty in representation and citation. Plagiarism comes in many forms: intentional, unintentional, and self-plagiarism. Only a few times in my career have students participated in the blatant sort of plagiarism of purchasing a paper or pasting large swaths of text from other sources into their own work. Interestingly, the directed freedom of topic selection often eliminates the possibility of even finding an essay on the same topic. More often, writers misunderstand the importance of attribution or simply do not take comprehensive or careful notes from their source material.

Citation formats often flummox students, and the proliferation of citation generators can hurt more than it helps because it complicates a simple process. Citation itself is actually incredibly democratic and generous, each citation offering an open door to the reader to access the same information as the writer. Making sure students have access to good style guides invites them to demystify citation. Most importantly, in order to build and maintain trust in a conversation, writers must represent their work and the evidence as honestly as possible. That means acknowledging the contributions of others, whether by attributing direct quotations or attributing information and ideas that are paraphrased. An honest representation of work also means that students who might want to "recycle" an old paper should talk with their instructors about how to do that well and in a way that promotes their own growth and thinking.

Approaching a conversation honestly means also that writers should not manipulate or excise data to their advantage. When my students encounter some piece of evidence or a situation that they might try to explain away or leave out because it wrinkles their argument, I ask them to leave it in, to wrestle with the tension. I give them permission not to win every aspect of their argument as long as the discussion helps move the conversation forward. The results are often refreshing and authentic.

Humility. A fourth ethical research principle is humility, which can and should be part of every step in the research process. Because *we do not yet know what we don't know,* approaching research with humility can suffuse the process with openness and make room for surprise. Chittister reminds us that humility is an *ease* with not knowing, which opens us to others and to life. She describes humility as "simply a basic awareness of my relationship to the world and my connectedness to all its circumstances."[10] Humility requires writers to assess the benefit of their work for the community and to consider the needs of their audience. Philosopher Martin Heidegger gave a brief lecture on the Greek word *logos* in which he contends that the noun form, so often associated with words and speaking, has a verb form, *legen,* which means "to lay before." In this sense of the word, speech requires gathering and sheltering, actions that imply planning and forethought.[11] The humility involved in admitting we don't yet know what we don't know invites "laying down" and "laying in." Most of us are familiar with the idea of *logos* as connected to words or logic, but this Heideggerian sense of *legen* appeals to me because good words and good logic require a listening posture that prepares us to enter fully into conversation.

Types of Attentive Listening

Relationship experts, therapists, and even business coaches advocate for attentive, "active" listening. In our writing, active listening can help us navigate complicated topics and communicate more

10. Chittister, *Wisdom Distilled from the Daily,* 65.
11. Heidegger, *Early Greek Thinking,* 62–66.

effectively with our readers. Therapist Nixaly Leonardo says active listening "enables us to connect genuinely with others, handle difficult situations, . . . and strengthen relationships."[12] She describes active listening as a combination of *passive, reflective,* and *critical listening.*[13]

As we approach a research conversation, it is often helpful to begin in *passive listening* where we listen receptively to our sources. At this stage, students have chosen topics, proposed a research question or motivating question, and identified some key contributors to the current conversation on the topic. Students need time to process all these voices, to read each one carefully without prejudice. Providing this time for students can feel wasteful of precious semester time—but modeling good reading strategies and offering opportunities to rank the readings in terms of accessibility or relevance can help students prioritize this passive listening phase of research.

After passive listening, writers can engage in *reflective listening.* Before even considering the rough draft, students compile an annotated bibliography. For each voice or source they encounter, they create a record of their listening, reflecting in summary what they hear the source saying. As an ongoing project, the annotated bibliography becomes an interactive tool where students process and catalog many voices in the conversation and prepare for analysis.

At this stage, it is helpful for students to understand and practice summary. One particularly helpful activity is a movie summary. We identify a movie that everyone has seen, and we usually end up with a Disney film (which oddly enough is almost always *Finding Nemo*). Grouping students in pairs, I ask them to summarize the movie in four sentences. One semester a group wrote:

> A clown fish loses his mother and then gets lost. His dad tries to find him. He makes a friend named Dory who has amnesia. At the end they are all reunited.

12. Leonardo, *Active Listening Techniques*, viii.
13. Leonardo, *Active Listening Techniques*, 4.

Another group wrote:

Finding Nemo follows the adventures of a young fish who has been stifled by his father's desire to protect him after his mother's tragic death. Once he sets out on his own, however, he realizes just how frightening the world is and how important it is to have friends and family to support you. After many adventures and mishaps, father and son are reunited. Both of them learn important lessons about what it means to live meaningful lives.

As the class hears from different groups, we draw on our collective knowledge of the film to discuss what the different summaries offer. The group that contributed the first of the summaries above astutely noted that it had been a long time since they had seen the film, so they did not have much passive listening knowledge to bring to their reflection on the movie. The second group observed that they omitted major events from their summary to focus on themes and larger narrative arcs. Though both summaries are technically accurate, they are clearly different. This exercise helps us understand that even in passive and reflective listening, we are making choices about what matters to us; what we "hear" may not be the same thing that someone else "hears" in a text. We may have to listen longer or listen again to be able to hear more accurately. Writer Wendell Berry contends in his essay "Standing by Words" "that language is communal and that its purpose is to tell the truth."[14] Reflective listening encourages us to tell the truth as best as we are able, and to make choices about what we are hearing in community rather than in isolation.

Taken together, passive and reflective listening make possible the next step: *critical listening*. As Leonardo puts it, "Critical listening requires the most effort. It involves processing a message while using your own judgments to differentiate between facts and opinions. It also requires creating your own analysis and opinions

14. Berry, *Standing by Words*, 26.

of the message being conveyed."[15] As the annotated bibliography comes together, students begin to trace responses and themes in the work. The best annotated bibliographies often facilitate their own "microdialogue" in which students use the annotations to indicate how each source might interact with other sources, where it deviates or aligns, and what threads they find interesting. Each year, writers comment that the annotated bibliography is by far the most helpful prewriting tool they have because it reveals intersections and contradictions that help develop vibrant conversation.

The annotated bibliography assignment is, of course, not unique to me or my classes, and I would encourage writers and instructors to tailor the exercise to their particular needs (appendix 3). Most handbook or internet descriptions of this type of assignment indicate that annotation should catalog the source's relevance, validity, or quality. While classifying and describing a source is perfectly acceptable, at early stages of the writing process the annotated bibliography should be useful to the *writer*, something I advocate in my version of the assignment. Seth, an economics major, used his annotated bibliography to track his own argument. In an annotation about a 2010 article on supply-side interventions, he wrote:

> This article attempts to find a correlation between decreased capital taxes and increased production and consumption of goods. They also conclude (like other sources) that reducing capital taxes results in an increase in economic activity. Such activity would come at an expense to the poor, as it would cause an increasing gap between rich and poor. The article is useful to me because it is a modern study of the policies Reagan implemented in the 1980s. Since I am also using an article written during the height of Reaganomics, an article looking back on the policy from a modern context will be important in forming my opinion.

15. Leonardo, *Active Listening Techniques*, 4.

Not only did Seth's citation summarize the source succinctly, but he also recognized the potential for dialogue between his sources. At this point in the process, he had a thesis, but he was still working on forming his opinion and was committed to listening to his research. Seth's writing was not just a "way of ordering perception," but as Verlyn Klinkenborg points out, a "way of reordering perception in a form peculiar to [his] discovery."[16] Seth did not simply collect a perfunctory list of sources; he instead began the process of reordering his own perceptions. As Seth discovered, approaching the annotated bibliography as a "microdialogue" within the research process puts many voices in conversation with the student's own project.

Evaluating Biases

Class discussions such as the bulletin board analysis and the summary exercise reveal that we all have particular biases. Biases are normal, and each one of us has a particular perspective or experience that colors our beliefs. Early in the class's discussion of the bulletin board, students were quick to criticize the institution and to stereotype groups of students, but given the opportunity to see from other points of view, most students modified their opinion. Biases cannot be eliminated, but they can be kept in check by humility and openness. Often, willingness to engage with another person's experience "changes people," as Zeldin writes, and if we begin our writing conversations willing to "emerge a slightly different person," we stand to gain more than we lose.[17] As our discussion of the bulletin board continued and we considered the pressures on the institution, students gained more empathy and were able to ask better questions. As we listened carefully to the experience of student athletes, students were able to see one group, athletes, as more complex. Empathy does not mean that

16. Klinkenborg, *Several Short Sentences about Writing*, 123.
17. Zeldin, *Conversation*, 3.

we cannot continue to disagree with a practice or an approach, but it helps us see more fully, research more comprehensively, and think more generously.

As students begin the critical listening phase of their research work, it is important to evaluate personal assumptions. Helping students understand their own point of reference can also help them engage the research with more objectivity. A quick point-of-reference checklist often helps writers to interrogate their own assumptions:

- Where do I live (country, state, community), and how might that influence my thinking?
- What are my religious and educational backgrounds, and how might they frame my response?
- What is my gender, ethnicity, or race, and how might that color my experience with this topic?
- What is my socioeconomic background, and how has that shaped my opportunities?
- How emotionally charged is this topic for me?

This time spent in reflection is not intended to change or criticize any of these frameworks, but rather simply to bring them into view. When writers at any level engage honestly with this process, it facilitates more honest engagement with the research. Participating in this kind of reflection also prepares students to listen more completely to those who might not have the same experiences.

Voices of Dissent

Biases often prevent us from hearing and listening to those who do not agree with us, but rarely are matters so contentious as to preclude common ground, though contemporary discourse might suggest otherwise. As journalist Stephen Miller writes, the "move toward diatribe and rant since the 1960s counterculture movement, which praised anger as 'authentic' and criticized 'civility as repressive,'" has impoverished our curiosity.[18] Writers have few models of arguments that include engaged listening, but many models of people talking over one another or slinging ad hominem insults instead of committing to true conversation. Rarely do we see debates in the public sphere center on empathy. Indeed, too much empathy with an opposing side in the political arena can result in attacks or accusations of weakness. But empathy can help us get to deeper and more meaningful understanding, though it requires what Krista Tippett, writer and host of the *On Being* podcast, calls "robust" or "gracious" listening. This type of listening comes from a place of curiosity and vulnerability. It involves being "willing to be surprised" and willingly engaging with ideas that might "unsettle your foundations"—those points of reference that dictate how we see and navigate the world.[19]

Another helpful exercise that harnesses curiosity and willingness to be surprised draws from the field of debate. In order to help students understand and accurately represent an opposing viewpoint, I ask them to listen to voices of dissent and demonstrate a complete and empathetic understanding of the opposing view or different experience. As Tippett also says, "I can disagree with your opinion, it turns out, but I cannot disagree with your experience."[20] I draw on a Rogerian style of debate that prioritizes understanding and compromise over winning. In a formal Rogerian debate, this type of understanding might look like Side A summarizing the opposing viewpoint to the satisfaction of Side B. To summarize a different viewpoint, writers must first identify the opposition to their chosen approach, which might not always be easy. It might

18. Miller, *Conversation*, xii.
19. Krista Tippett, interview by Max Linsky, *Longform* (podcast), October 12, 2016, https://longform.org/posts/longform-podcast-215-krista-tippett.
20. Tippett, *Becoming Wise*, 22.

be hard for Norma, the student writing about machismo, to find any common ground with proponents of historical masculinity or those with strong religious convictions regarding gender roles. It might also be easy for her to reject those views out of hand, but careful research of those objections might offer a more sympathetic portrait of those beliefs. As she discovered in her own summary, many men experience severe repercussions for abandoning machismo norms, which helped her understand their opposition more completely and frame a more informed response to that opposition. This exercise creates empathy, and as in a debate, it also helps students frame more sound, precise rebuttals.

For Chittister, disciplined, engaged listening requires "listening to all of life and learning to respond to each of its dimensions wholly and with integrity."[21] Holly, a political science major, proposed an essay on the minimum wage. She planned to argue that raising the minimum wage was unnecessary and potentially detrimental to business owners. But as she spent time with her research—listening to the stories of those impacted by a stagnant wage, evaluating the data, and tracing economic impacts—something amazing happened. She began to see more than one side of the issue. Holly's core values remained intact, but she was able to make a more nuanced and empathetic argument—synthesizing the opposing sides by proposing instead a moderate wage hike, among other reforms. Holly's argument expanded; it might even be fair to say her world expanded because she was willing to be "called beyond" herself.[22] As she prepares to graduate and is already moving into a political life, I have no doubt that she will approach her work with the same empathy. Would that all our politicians were willing to risk being changed in that way.

A counterargument summary could take many forms. In my own classes, I ask first-year writers to complete a more comprehensive

21. Chittister, *Wisdom Distilled from the Daily*, 16.
22. Chittister, *Wisdom Distilled from the Daily*, 15.

summary. First-year composition culminates in a traditional issue argument essay, which makes the counterargument summary even more important for writers who may not have experience empathizing with the opposition. For these students, I require that they summarize the opposing position and, in the Rogerian style, defend it using evidence. They must conclude the summary with a paragraph reflecting on the common ground they find with the opposing argument. This work may or may not make it into their actual essay, but it infuses their writing with such depth that it is a worthwhile exercise to develop empathy and a broader perspective. For the second-year writers who are researching in their field, understanding the many voices in a field of study brings similar depth. I ask them to find at least one scholar who disagrees with their own thesis, to read that scholar's work (or a sample of it), and to summarize it carefully. As the final step, I ask them to find points of agreement or potential synthesis, write a rebuttal, and offer a new path forward. Though this exercise is less comprehensive, its specificity often facilitates a more intimate and purposeful connection with an opposing voice.

Listening well to others requires an open mental posture (and an open physical posture, for that matter—imagine trying to talk with someone whose crossed arms and furrowed brow signal their resistance). Drawing on Heidegger's foundation, philosopher H. G. Gadamer emphasizes that "anyone who listens is fundamentally open. Without this kind of openness to one another there is no genuine human relationship. Belonging together always also means being able to listen to one another."[23] Heidegger recognized the fundamental relationship between speaking and listening, the moment of "laying in" before we could set forth our ideas. Gadamer extends this relationship beyond the spoken word to our interactions with one another. Thinking about openness in writing (even and especially undergraduate writing) as the site for "genuine human relationship" has the potential to transform our writing

23. Gadamer, *Truth and Method*, 326.

and our perception of that writing. Being curious enough to ask an evocative question and humble enough to listen makes such openness a possibility. Philosophers, climate scientists, nuns, and even Tarantino gangsters agree that listening, even though it isn't easy, is crucial to remain in conversation with the world and with those around us.

three

Be Relatable

When my students listed the word "relatable" as a marker of good conversation, I asked for clarification, not because I did not agree, but because it was such an apt description of what makes written and personal conversations work. One young man explained, "It's a way into the writing," a lovely description of the generosity involved in being relatable. Being relatable is deeply related to curiosity and listening well, and it is, perhaps unsurprisingly, equally important to writers and readers. Opening a door into our writing is less about knowing the audience (though relating to an audience is important) than it is about being authentic. Years ago, when I was working on my dissertation, I sent off a chapter draft to my advisor. He returned it noting that my analysis and research worked, but that the writing was stiff and disconnected. Only after I reassessed why I was writing the chapter and how I related to the topic was I able to find a "way in." Understanding my own connection and motivation to write opened that door for me *and* my readers.

Thinking about an audience can be a bit tricky for writers. Of course, we should consider that potential reader; I'm always asking

my students to be gracious to their audience. But too much audience anticipation can paralyze any writer and produce a stilted,
inauthentic voice. In my dissertation I was so intent on writing
for some faceless academic audience that I lost a sense of my
own voice, of my own stake in the writing. One of my colleagues,
a professor of history and humanities, says he likes to imagine
his father, an industry chemist with a PhD in chemistry, as part
of his audience. That is, though my colleague might be writing
about sixteenth-century church history, he wants his father to have
access to his writing. His well-educated father may not have the
background to appreciate all aspects of the argument, but he can
follow that path into the writing because my colleague's generosity
assumes ignorance but not stupidity.

Writing relatably means we explain jargon or replace it with accessible language; it means we explain technical terms and provide
context; and it means we avoid dictionary references to common
words, or an encyclopedic history of the subject that might conde-
scend to readers. Annie Dillard, in her book *The Writing Life,* says:

> Write as if you were dying. At the same time, assume you write for
> an audience consisting solely of terminal patients. That is, after all,
> the case. What would you begin writing if you knew you would die
> soon? What could you say to a dying person that would not enrage
> by its triviality?[1]

Dillard's directive might seem a bit dramatic for an introductory
composition classroom, but it is a fitting call to clarity and specificity and also a helpful vision of a writing audience. Rather than
picturing a be-gowned academic committee, imagining instead
how to make the most of an audience's time (and our own) can
infuse our writing with purpose.

Relating to readers, which demonstrates goodwill toward the
audience, first takes shape in the writing as being connected to

1. Dillard, *Writing Life,* 68.

the topic itself. Inevitably, and more so now that the age gap between me and my students exceeds two decades, students choose to write about topics that are more germane to them than to me. Sometimes, I have little context for their interests, but when students take the time to "find a way in" for themselves and for me, I often come away having learned and grown from their work. When my daughter was younger, she would often begin talking without context, leaving the rest of us puzzling through her connections. When asked for clarification, she would patiently explain her associations—the steak we were eating made her think of the barbeque we hosted, which made her think of summer, which made her think of swimming, which made her think of a trip to the beach. These days, she is an accomplished conversationalist who takes care to contextualize, ask insightful questions, and invite others into her observations, but these skills only came through practice. Writers, too, can inadvertently leave readers struggling to bridge leaps of logic on their own, and they bear the same responsibility for ensuring that their audience has the tools necessary to relate to and participate in the conversation.

My graduate school professors often referenced "unpacking" texts and thoughts. Whatever the merits of the phrase, it stayed with me as a useful metaphor. When I am confused by what feels like a huge leap or shift, I ask students how they arrived at their statement. I often ask them if they have information in their heads that they have not shared on the page. Almost always, the answer is yes. Sometimes they have simply assumed the reader has the same information, like my daughter. Sometimes they do not know how to include all the background needed without overwhelming the prose. Either way, the hard work of unpacking, of teasing apart our writing as we might the contents of an overstuffed suitcase, helps the reader arrive at the destination with clarity of purpose. Cognitive scientist Steven Pinker observes that "readers know a lot less about your subject than you think they do, and unless you keep track of what you know that they don't, you are guaranteed to confuse them."[2] He references the "curse of knowledge," a reluctance to believe that others do not approach a topic with the same understanding or experience that we do, and he observes that "when we know something well, we don't realize how abstractly we think about it."[3] Unpacking our knowledge extends an invitation to readers to explore the topic together.

Thanks to student writing, I have learned about the impact of travel sports teams on families, the role of women in engineering, and the admirable intersectionality of video games. Each year, students surprise and delight me with their interests, and what is more, we discover common ground in these topics. Reece, a history major with military ambitions and a passion for duck hunting, wrote so passionately about the impact of climate change on duck migration patterns that despite having little else in common (I have never shot a gun and could likely only distinguish Daffy from Donald with certainty), we continue to engage in stimulating conversations about our shared concern for climate change, even after the course has ended. Reece chose a topic that interested him, but he took care to find a way in for his readers, which meant tempering assumptions about their experience and considering carefully how his "curse of knowledge" might bias or eclipse his presentation.

Opening the Door: Introductions

Determining a formal "way in" to a topic stymies writers of all kinds. In my classes we reference the introduction image often cited by writing teachers of the upside-down funnel, which moves us gradually from a general introduction to a more specific thesis. But even those terms—general to specific—do not always clarify the goal of an introduction for writers. We also consider the introduction as a toolbox for moving through the rest of the essay. We might list five research keywords and work to incorporate those

2. Pinker, *Sense of Style*, 63.
3. Pinker, *Sense of Style*, 67.

concepts into the introduction. We also play a topic introduction "dating game" in which students have only a minute to succinctly introduce their topic to a partner. Rarely does anyone begin with a Merriam-Webster definition of a word or with a Wikipedia history of the topic. Just as in a personal conversation, introducing a topic need not start at the beginning of time or with a basic definition of terms, but with those details we most need to know or with information that makes a connection. Different kinds of writing and different topics require different techniques to connect with readers and find points of entry, and identifying these universally *unhelpful* techniques helps writers see the purpose and potential of introductory work.

Most writers have had some exposure to introduction techniques that engage readers (often called "hooks"), and many of those techniques can be helpful if used intentionally and with reflection. Sometimes students begin with quotations, which is not a bad approach if the quotation is contextualized and connected well to the topic. Even if the quotation is perfect, however, the speaker should fit the ethos of the writing. If a search of the internet for "quotations about fishing" leads to an excellent quotation, but the life and work of the speaker is at odds with the topic, the quotation might do more harm than good in setting up the writing. That is, if the writer wants to argue for conservation and the quotation comes from a person who actively works against conservation, the hook compromises the thesis. Quotations that provide the best entry to a topic often emanate from the research itself, from work the writer has engaged deeply rather than those found in a cursory internet search.

Sometimes writers begin with a startling fact, some almost unbelievable piece of information guaranteed to engage a reader's attention. I recently read a book about climate change that begins with such overwhelming statistics that I could barely believe their validity. So great was their impact that before I even finished the first page, I had to sit with the gravity of those numbers. I immediately turned to the bibliography to see when and how those statistics were obtained. The author had provided a clear pathway to his research, which made his startling introduction even more powerful. Writers have a responsibility to deploy information ethically by confirming the origin and context of such staggering information if they want to connect with readers.

Another entry point to a topic, and one that composition students are often surprised to find at their disposal, is the personal story or anecdote. Though the technique itself is not new, and it is used as an entry point for everything from sermons to TED Talks, most composition students have never considered using an anecdote to connect to their topic or their readers. In part, this hesitancy stems from a well-meaning prohibition early writers often encounter: don't use the first person in expository writing. Using the first person can be quite effective in research and analytical writing, but it requires some discernment to avoid an entire argument based on nothing but "I believe" statements. While supporting an argument requires more than a personal belief, making a first-person association can create a powerful motivation to connect with the topic. The first section of the research proposal template that I give my composition students (appendix 2) asks them to consider their personal connection and motivation to the topic, and it can be a good resource in helping them develop their personal connection to the topic later in their writing.

Finding the right story, like deploying the first person, requires some practice and prudence, as well as an evaluation of the story's merits.

- Is the story true?
- Will it condense well?
- Is the story mine to tell?
- Is the story relevant?

These kinds of introductions often require more than one paragraph, wherein the story works as a sort of introduction to the introduction. Writers must balance the overall weight of the introduction with the rest of the essay. I ask writers to think of their projects in percentages—if a project will range from ten to twelve pages, the introduction may only constitute 15 percent, or approximately one and a half pages. Because stories can overwhelm and prolong an introduction, writers need to avoid an overly slow unspooling of their anecdote.

Sometimes writers recount their own experience and sometimes they recount an experience involving a close relative or friend, which is also acceptable. Not all stories need to be distinctly personal, but recounting someone else's experience involves consent and skill. The minister at a local church, a great storyteller, regularly pays his daughters if he uses stories about them in his sermons. If he uses another person's experience to illustrate his argument, he makes a point to ask their permission and provide context for the story's purpose. A person might be perfectly amenable to their experience being used as a positive illustration but less enthusiastic about being a cautionary tale. Either way, telling someone else's story should be approached with care to represent details as accurately and objectively as possible. In the absence of a good personal story, sometimes writers might be tempted to create a hypothetical scenario to set up their thesis. Too often, though, the hypothetical anecdote veers toward fallacy or an excess of pathos. Readers gravitate toward stories, and if the writer reveals that a story is hypothetical, it can feel like a sort of mini-betrayal to have invested in a narrative only to find out it was an exercise in what-ifs. Similarly, some types of research, such as case studies, will offer compelling personal accounts. While such stories might perfectly illustrate the thesis and provide an interesting connection, they are better used as examples or evidence rather than an entry to the writer's own research. A true, personal story summarized to balance anecdote with tools for the introduction toolbox creates a meaningful connection to the topic.

Finally, an effective anecdote should be relevant to the main thesis. Sometimes writers become attached to a story, and it may well have motivated their initial research, but as the idea evolves the story no longer sets up the topic seamlessly. In such cases, the story sets up an expectation that the thesis does not fulfill, and readers are left confused instead of connected. Even when revision reveals that a story no longer fits, the process of finding a way in for the writer is ultimately valuable. Not all research writing will benefit from a story, but all writers can benefit from that personal connection to their research.

Marking the Path: Thesis Statements

If the introduction itself provides a "way in" to the topic, the thesis provides a "way in" to the argument itself. A thesis should clearly and concisely indicate the writer's direction and position the writer in the conversation. A thesis statement's length and style vary in relation to the writing itself. My colleague and I were researching and writing our dissertations at the same time, and occasionally we would emerge from our offices and meet in the hallway to shake off the fog of long writing days. Our go-to question was "One sentence, no semicolons?" What we meant by that question was "Are you able to articulate your project in a single, simple sentence yet?" A dissertation-length argument need not be encapsulated in a single, simple sentence, but the ability to render it so succinctly meant that we were finally comfortable enough with our own work that we could relate it easily to those outside our academic fields. Developing ease with a topic often happens gradually, and a thesis may (and often does) evolve over the course of our research. Drafting a working thesis helps point writers in the right direction, while the research process helps hone and polish the argument.

Once writers have developed a research proposal, they can draw on their research problem and questions to help craft a thesis. Even if they have not completed a research proposal, beginning with a question invites the writer to listen before positing a thesis. After developing a research question, a writer might ask:

- What do I want to say in response to this question?
- What does the research say in response to this question?
- How might I synthesize the research and contribute to the conversation surrounding this topic?

This process can take a long time or a little time, depending on how confident the writer is in the material. Because working thesis statements are malleable, if the argument shifts as the writer synthesizes the research, the thesis can and should shift as well. As always, working through an example to model the process makes it more accessible and concrete. What follows is a class response (hence the use of the plural "we") to one of the model research questions from the CFP (appendix 1):

A sample research problem:[4]

Reliable information is vital to democracy, but the news business is dying. Local news, in particular, is struggling to survive in twenty-first-century America. Nearly 2,000 newspapers have gone out of business in the last fifteen years. Half of all news industry jobs have disappeared. There are now more than 1,300 "news deserts" in the US, where citizens have no regular information about their communities. Even where newspapers continue to exist, coverage is noticeably thinner. More than 1,000 newspapers have cut their reporting staff in half, and one study found that 20 percent of small newspapers don't carry any local news on a given day. National headlines, cable TV commentary, and Internet clickbait don't make up the difference. Some of the negative effects are already visible. Voting participation declines in news deserts, while taxes go up and boondoggles proliferate. Without anyone to report it, corruption runs rampant in county court houses, police departments, school

4. Sample problem and question contributed by Dr. Daniel Silliman.

boards, and city halls. Nationally, the country faces a rapid rise in political polarization, fake news, and conspiracy theories.

Sample research questions:

> Can the news business be radically reimagined? Should we change how we think about "news," or "local," or develop new funding models? Are there alternative financial approaches that would work in modern America? Are there new modes of journalism—citizen journalism, nonprofit journalism, partisan watchdog groups—that could provide people the information they need to safeguard a healthy, thriving democracy?

After considering these questions and the preliminary research carefully, the class responded to the question "What do we want to say?":

> We want to argue that the importance of clear-eyed journalism and commitment to objectivity is vital to a healthy dialogue and democracy. We want to examine the success of alternative media outlets and suggest some potential paths forward, especially for "news deserts." We see this problem in TN, in which 68 of 95 counties have only 1 local news source and 4 of 95 counties have no local news source at all.[5]

Articulating what we wanted to say revealed that we needed more information to help frame a hypothesis. We did more cursory research in class and considered again: What does the research say? Here are the class's notes:

- Traditional news organizations in decline
- "Echo chamber" creates stress and division

---

5. Statistics taken from Penelope Muse Abernathy, "The Expanding News Desert," University of North Carolina Hussman School of Journalism and Media, accessed August 16, 2022, https://www.usnewsdeserts.com/states/tennessee.

- Value in ethical, objective reporting
- More people valuing biased reporting
- News deserts have negative impact on communities (voting decline and misinformation)
- Journalism nonprofits benefit local news (like ProPublica)
- Many local news organizations are owned by only a handful of national companies

Once we considered the new information, we began asking: How might we synthesize the research, focus our argument, and contribute to the conversation? Again, the class notes:

- Rethinking how news is delivered, but *not changing* high standards of journalism. Introduce an objective third party or tool to help deliver news?
- We care about political reconciliation and the decline of trust in the journalists in the United States. Communicating/rating news outlets?
- We want to focus on a local impact to make the topic more accessible.

Finally, we worked together to develop a working thesis that would direct our efforts and shape our project:

Developing a relationship with organizations like the ProPublica Local Reporting Network could not only alleviate the news deserts in Tennessee, but it could develop interest in non- or bipartisan conversations that begin in local events.

This process took an entire class period as we reflected together on the question, conducted research in groups, and developed potential thesis statements together. This final class thesis has strong potential, and it could not have been developed without time to reflect on and engage with the research.

The thesis statement above avoids some of the ineffective strate-gies often associated with thesis writing, such as metadiscourse, scapegoat language, and itemized "prongs." In personal conver-sation, we rarely (if ever) have occasion to state *that* we are talk-ing. We do not say to someone, "In this conversation, I will state some facts and then respond to you." Writers default to this type of metadiscourse all the time, though it rarely accomplishes any-thing. I theorize that we do this out of a misguided attempt to relate to readers (Look, I'm human and I'm writing this essay!) or an attempt to delay the argument. Either way, metadiscourse rarely accomplishes much. I ask students to focus instead on the substance of their argument, to assume that readers know they are reading an essay, and to allow their introductory work to connect them to their audience.

"Scapegoat language"—words such as "people" or "society" or "the church" or "culture"—offers monolithic ideas to which writers might ascribe all manner of good or bad qualities. George Orwell, in his essay "Politics and the English Language," describes this type of language as meaningless because "it has no discoverable object."[6] Orwell criticizes these abstract, meaningless words as lazy and sometimes dangerous. Thinking carefully and specifically about each word in the thesis helps us to avoid crafting a straw-man argument. In a thesis statement especially, language connected to "discoverable objects" better positions the reader and the writer to enter the argument.

And finally, the itemized prong—typically a "three-prong thesis"—is a remnant of the five-paragraph essay construct. As a learning tool, the three-prong thesis can benefit students by en-couraging organization and follow-through, but the three-prong thesis does not often hold up well for longer or more complex argu-ments. In most cases, the three-prong argument tends to focus on three major concepts—ideas that could easily bear the scrutiny of many paragraphs, sometimes pages. And as is the case in nearly

6. Orwell, "Politics and the English Language," 359.

all writing, the more general the argument, the less there is to say about it. In many cases, a three-prong argument is repetitive. Take, for example, the following sentence:

> The American Government should increase funding for cancer research because cancer deaths continue to increase (Prong 1), innovative treatments require support (Prong 2), and better understanding of cancer will result in better preventative care (Prong 3).

Prong 1 is not actually part of the argument, but is, instead, part of the problem. This information could be stated as part of the introduction or even as a motivating part of the thesis ("Because cancer deaths . . ."). Prong 2 is connected to Prong 3, and together, they reveal the ultimate argument of the thesis: that funding research for better preventative care and treatment could reduce both deaths and the trauma of treatment. The essay would then shift toward a more purposeful exploration of how to secure and promote the necessary funding. The three-prong argument can be a useful entry for writers, however, and if that is where they need to begin, I encourage them to do so, but I also encourage them to evaluate each prong for its purpose and relation to their argument. After this type of review, most writers arrive at a more specific working thesis that shepherds all parties into their argument.

Draft Discussions: Peer Review

Once writers have introduced their topic and developed a thesis, the drafting process can begin in earnest. I ask students to conduct peer review during many stages of the writing process and again once the draft is complete. Putting drafts into real conversation makes many writers nervous. Something about committing words to a page and putting them into the world seems riskier than simply speaking an opinion, and engaging with real readers rather than hypothetical readers makes some writers nervous. Though it can feel risky, peer review begins the process of extending the research dialogue beyond the page itself, and certainly beyond my desk. Students have commented that conversations both with me and with their peers help them assess the effect of their drafts. Peer review is not to be confused with editing, and I ask my own students not to mark edits at all, and instead to focus on the argument itself. In class we allot time to read their essays, express reactions, and offer feedback. Divorced from the task of editing, writers react to the argument and its structure honestly and with compassion, which always impresses me. Perhaps tempering criticism with compassion seems only appropriate and natural after having invested the same time and effort in their own projects. I require teams of two to read together, discussing the paper in conversation and providing detailed feedback for the writers. The nuance and high quality of student conversation reflects their deep investment in the process. They may not know exactly how to fix what is broken, but they do recognize effective and ineffective arguments. As they articulate their reactions to their peers' work, they are also more likely to engage productively with their own writing.

Over the years, I have experimented with dozens of peer review approaches, some complicated, some simple, some more successful than others. In a composition-as-conversation classroom, however, peer review can model the intentional dialogue and meaningful interactions that will serve students well as they continue to write and revise. Prioritizing relationships both among students and with the material facilitates a far more successful peer review process than simply marking mistakes. I have found that whatever approach I choose, four basic elements support productive peer review:

- modeling and expectations
- review guides
- ample time to read
- reflection and discussion

Modeling and Expectations

Student experience with peer review may vary widely, and often those experiences may not have been positive. If students understand the writing process as a conversation, then peer review can and should be part of that conversation. Taking time to make sure writers know how to relate to one another as reviewers through a peer interview can improve their feedback significantly (appendix 4). After facilitating these peer relationships in the interview, using a sample paper to model response and discussion can also be helpful. Setting expectations for the activity also improves the experience. For example, I expect peer reviewers to engage with the paper throughout the margins, to offer a response to the work, and to ask questions of the writer. Offering clear guidelines for the allotted time prevents readers from rushing through the work. I invite students who finish quickly to read the paper as many times as they are able, or to read the introduction and conclusion side by side. Phones and computers are stowed away until the process is complete.

Review Guides

Providing a peer review guide (appendix 4) trains writers to ask content questions of their peer's work instead of focusing on editing. Guides are helpful, but ultimately, I care more about the interaction than the guide, and I do not collect or grade them. Shorter guides tend to be less intimidating for students, and assignment-specific guides help focus the review. Giving students an opportunity to craft their own question for reviewers, either as part of the formal guide or during the peer interview process, encourages writers and reviewers to invest in the experience. Though each peer review guide has a similar focus, tailoring specific tasks or questions to the writing assignment can elicit purposeful feedback from reviewers.

Ample Time to Read

Reading essays takes time and concentration. Though I prefer to keep the entire peer review process in the classroom, for longer papers especially, students need more time to engage with the work. Course management software and digital communication make out-of-class reading exchanges easier, though not always seamless or consistent, which is why offering more class time can be fruitful. For many years, I offered only one class period for peer review, but providing more time for reading decompresses the process, encourages deeper engagement, and results in better feedback. In the absence of more class time or access to course management software, peer review deep dives into specific sections of a long paper can also yield meaningful feedback.

A mistake I made for many years was to assume that peer review was a monolithic process unrelated to the individual writers and assignment. Each writing assignment requires different peer review parameters because peer review should fit the assignment and the group of writers. I tweak my review guides every year and experiment with different configurations. For example, one year, anonymous peer review guides were wildly successful—eliciting strong feedback and enthusiastic participation. Just a year later, students echoed the same kind of anonymous, mean-spirited behavior seen in online comment sections in these reviews. Furthermore, in a conversation-focused classroom, the students themselves began to desire meaningful conversations. When we switched to a one-on-one conversational format mid-semester, the outcomes improved dramatically. The peer interview helps students invest in one another's work no matter what kind of guide they use.

Though it is not perfect, peer review is a powerful conversational process that permits students to relate to one another's work and to see their own work more clearly. One student recently completed an introduction peer review, and she realized that after reading other students' work, her own entry, though effective, needed to be tightened. Peer review exposed her to other introduction approaches, and it helped her read her own introduction more objectively.

Reflection and Discussion

One of the most important benefits of ample time for peer review is the opportunity for reflection and conferencing. Ethicist Ellen Ott Marshall writes that the "impulse to defend our perspective, justify our position, rationalize our actions, or assert our own point of view leads us to erroneous understanding."[7] Dedicating time for reflection helps students create "space to receive [criticism]" even if it is uncomfortable.[8] When I am not conducting anonymous peer reviews, I allot time in the process for student reviewers to conference with student writers. Instead of handing back drafts with marks on them, the students engage in lively and productive conversations about their work. When I am conducting anonymous peer reviews, I allot time for writers to review their feedback in class, to begin thinking about how they will respond to that feedback, and to ask for clarification before they leave. In personal conversational experiences, it can be difficult to sit with criticism, even when it is offered constructively. Making the effort to consider improvement requires vulnerability, and in the writing classroom, being vulnerable as a group can help motivate a confident and receptive approach to criticism. By making reflection a part of our practice, students come to welcome that constructive criticism instead of dreading it.

A Relatable Conversation

Finding a relatable way into our writing is an act of generosity and respect. Being relatable in conversation and in writing involves respecting your dialogue partner, the subject, the evidence,

7. Marshall, *Introduction to Christian Ethics*, 150.
8. Marshall, *Introduction to Christian Ethics*, 149.

and yourself; it involves approaching writing as an opportunity to develop relationships instead of scoring points or being right. The writing process itself offers many opportunities to practice relatability, from the point of entry to the eventual conversation with a reading partner. As we work to develop connections to our material and to our audience, we develop an authenticity in our writing voice. Recently, a student chose a topic that interested him, but soon recognized that he did not have the time to develop sufficiently deep connections. Though he had conducted strong research, he realized that it would take many more months of reading to develop enough familiarity with the topic to create a path into it for his readers. He wisely narrowed his topic to a much more specific branch of that field and saved the broader topic for another day. His final project made a compelling argument, all the more so because in the early stages of drafting he recognized the need for relatability. Being relatable is not the same thing as being liked or being fashionable; rather, being relatable upholds those same principles of listening, attention, and curiosity that bring about genuine dialogue. Being vulnerable enough to cultivate an authentic connection to our material encourages others to care about the conversation too.

four

Be on Topic

One unexpectedly warm late November Saturday, my children and I decided to tackle a different trail at one of our favorite mountain hiking spots. We hike this mountain frequently, so after cursorily skimming the hike description, we set out, eager to see the promised vista in all its fall glory. We confidently blazed the steep, overgrown trail, and after a mile or so, we expected some indication of our progress. The trail's markers, however, were infrequent and faint, and with each step our confidence began to ebb. After several more miles, we had to admit, a bit sheepishly, that we were lost. Hot and frustrated, we pointed ourselves back toward the car, disappointed and eager to return home. We knew where we wanted to be, but we simply could not find our way.

Staying on topic is a little like our experience on that mountain, which of course involves staying on the path, but which also means signaling that path well. Part of our problem was our overconfidence. We assumed our frequent visits would translate to familiarity even though we had never hiked that trail, and those assumptions led us to believe our minimal preparation would carry us through. Writers face similar pitfalls. Sometimes we fail to signal the direction of our discussion, or we promise a discussion that never materializes. Or perhaps we blaze into a discussion overconfident and underprepared, leading to confusion and frustration for everyone. As an indication of a good conversation, being on topic means more than finding the way from point A to point B. Writers do need to provide clear paths through their argument, but they also need to proceed consistently, developing their own voices along the way.

Writers who stay on topic navigate the ebb and flow of a conversation, introducing, analyzing, and extending ideas. Such work means sometimes listening, sometimes responding, but always working to move the conversation forward by synthesizing multiple viewpoints and voices into a clear argument, a decidedly difficult task. Each new voice can distract from the original intent if not carefully placed in conversation. The work of outlining and annotating sources helps contextualize those voices, but researchers need to take careful notes as well. One of the most useful skills my high school English teacher imparted to me was the importance of careful notetaking. He emphasized rigorous bibliographies and citations, not for fear of plagiarism (though I am sure that was part of it) but so that we would be able to locate those sources easily as we drafted. He required notecards and bibliography cards, and that visual connection between the notes I was taking and their original "source" card stayed with me as a lifelong research practice. One of my favorite parts of that process was positioning the notecard bearing my claim in the middle of the table and organizing all the different notecards around my central idea. Physically juxtaposing my ideas with those of other scholars and in conversation with the evidence inspired new ideas and better understanding. Though I now gravitate toward spiral-bound notebooks, my research process is ultimately the same. Whatever the approach, all writers need an organizing strategy to help corral and process their research.

Engaging Evidence: Taking Notes

In my writing classroom, students complete "micro-assignments," low-stakes assignments designed to move them toward their eventual draft. Before we begin working in earnest on our research, students complete a notetaking micro-assignment intended to launch them toward good research practices. The assignment requires:

- the bibliographic citation
- an academic summary of the source
- one potentially useful quotation, cited appropriately
- three key points, paraphrased and cited appropriately, with a brief reflection on their salience
- the annotated source article

A notetaking activity such as this gives writers an opportunity to practice engaging with research and also encourages them to begin developing their own voice, an important part of developing consistency.

As writers take notes from their research, they become more familiar with the material. Some evidence will need to be quoted directly, but much of it can be paraphrased and cited appropriately. Citing evidence involves introducing and balancing the tenor of someone else's voice, often the voice of a scholar or expert in the subject. The work of paraphrasing ensures that writers know the evidence intimately enough to render it in their own voice.

In conjunction with selective quotation in the form of partial quotations, ellipsed quotations, or quoted phrases, paraphrasing can maintain the writer's voice with consistency. Style guides abound with directions about when and how to use quotations, and I highly recommend consulting a guide about the *mechanics* of quotation. The *art* of quotation can be further developed using strong conversational skills. When we quote others in conversation, we draw on their good reputations, and we do so in a social contract to represent them accurately. One of the quickest paths to discord is to misrepresent a friend for personal gain while in conversation with someone else. Sometimes, in order to avoid this pitfall, we might be tempted to indicate that "many" people agree with our claim. We do seem to be living in an age of "many," in which collective agreement signals strength, if not (dubious) veracity. In personal conversations full of mutuality and respect, few of us would resort to an unknown and unnamed "many," but in moments of intellectual friction or outright disagreement, especially when two parties have not cultivated mutuality, the tendency toward "many" can lead to sloppy, unfocused arguments. Consider the difference between these two sentences:

> Many people agree with the city's decision to restructure the city's transit system.

> Amir Bradshaw, leader of the City Community Service Board, and Frances Shoals, the library director, both support the plan to restructure the city's transit system.

The first example offers no context for the agreement, nor does it anticipate the people who might disagree. The second example cites two city leaders whose constituents rely on public transit, and thus have a high stake in a careful approach; in this case, their credentials have more impact than the quantity of those who agree or disagree. This second example also frames a dialogue, in which the next steps might be to cite the leaders' reasons and the context of their agreement. Citing a specific and credible person, in writing and in personal conversation, brings gravity and clarity to a claim that can preemptively dispel disagreement or generate new discussion for even stronger outcomes.

Corralling the Conversation: Outlines and Topic Threads

Staying on topic begins with clear direction. The research proposal can provide a good foundation, but outlines can offer even more detail and structure. Outlines can be formal or informal, but they should always be flexible and specific. Many writers find outlines to be useless because outlines that include only markers of content are indeed useless. An outline that includes in its major headings words such as "introduction" or "section 1" or "conclusion" does not clarify or organize thinking. Writers who instead identify actual topics to be introduced, state claims to be made, and include references to evidence will have an easier time drafting in general, and a far easier time staying on topic. Writing an outline after completing a proposal, compiling an annotated bibliography, and working through a thesis encourages this specificity. Like the annotated bibliography, an outline should be meaningful to the writer as a form of initial dialogue, an ideal itinerary for their discussion. As an instructor, I care far more about the outline's functional practicality than I do about its format.

Writers approach the outline structure in many different ways: traditional roman numerals, bulleted lists, section sketches, and various hybrids. No matter the style, I ask writers to include in each section of the outline clear guiding ideas, supporting details, and references to evidence. I ask them to decide how much room they want to make for each part of their discussion. To repeat a point made in chapter 3, thinking about a writing assignment in terms of percentages can help illuminate its organization. If the writer expects to write roughly four thousand words, or approximately fifteen pages, what percentage of those words should be given to introducing? To background? To counterarguing? While this process might not appeal to all writers, for many, it clarifies their planning. Especially for longer writing projects, sectioned outlines and percentages can help writers envision distinct elements of the argument and their connection to the overarching claim. Whatever form it takes, the outline offers a touchstone during the drafting process, a path back through the forest.

Staying on topic requires the organization provided by outlines and proposals, but it also requires forecasting that organization within the draft itself. In shorter essays, writers might offer a new topic claim in each paragraph, a sort of mini-claim derived from the thesis. In longer works, tying sections together with topic threads promotes deeper discussion. Topic threads imply continuity, and even if each paragraph takes on a slightly different element of the claim or simply transitions to further discussion, the construction holds together. Each paragraph explores and synthesizes evidence, increasing the potential dialogue opportunities.

Writers must take these opportunities to further the conversation, making meaning with their responses. Too often, writers pass up this opportunity, instead following a piece of evidence with some version of "this quote shows" or "this quote means." In personal conversations, we would quickly tire of a dialogue partner who simply repeated or summarized every point we made. ("Hey Amy, I bought two tickets to the concert. This statement means I will have two seats at the concert.") We crave thoughtful and studied responses to our ideas, and writers who bring this practice into their work elevate their discourse. For example, here are four ways a writer could follow up on a direct quotation that delivers evidence that "10 percent of all school children eat their only healthy meal at school":

This quote shows that many children rely on school lunches.

This quote means that school lunches are important.

Because so many children rely on school lunches, these lunches need to be appealing and healthy.

In the summer, then, these children have fewer food options, and community lunch programs could fill the gap.

A writer who responds with the first or second example misses a chance to further the conversation. In the latter two responses, the writer has elevated the thinking and moved the conversation forward toward a claim. Interestingly, that one piece of evidence could be applied fairly to several different types of claims about school lunches, because a piece of evidence may not have a fixed application. In my writing classes, I often trace the journey from "observation" to "making meaning," where meaning is understood as observation or knowledge made active. Making meaning involves bringing wholeness or purpose to a perspective, which can only happen with careful listening and consideration. School lunch data carries little meaning until it sparks a connection, an application, and ultimately, action or a call to action. Making meaning of our interactions with the evidence is the work of thoughtful conversations.

Artful Architecture: Sustaining Topicality

Topic threads coupled with thoughtful synthesis create an overall architecture for writing that explores and sustains a thesis. There are many metaphors for writing, such as the hamburger model, which asks writers to think of the introduction and conclusion as bread and the essay body as the meat patty, but many such metaphors are incomplete in some way. Over the years, I have found that the image of a Christmas tree can help students envision the work of the thesis and the topic threads throughout the writing. At the top, sparkling with invitation and serving as a guiding light, is the star: the introduction. When I illustrate the tree in my classes, using my admittedly poor artistic skills, I render the star as an inverted triangle to signify the movement toward a specific thesis. I draw the trunk of the tree next, a stabilizing thesis from which grow the branches of discussion. Then I add layers of branches, the traditional Christmas tree triangle shapes that begin in a clear topic thread and swell to synthesis and conclusion in each section, adding ornamentation and lights to indicate evidence, response, and style. And finally, I add a single present at the base of the tree to represent the conclusion, a parting gift from the writer for readers to consider and take with them. This image, though almost certainly reductive, helps writers envision the structure of their work and maybe even connect it to a tradition of gifting and celebration. Much like the Christmas holiday itself, with its tradition of Advent and anticipation, staying on topic does not happen all at once, but instead requires familiarity, creativity, and careful planning. While conversationalists might be forgiven for doubling back or straying from the original idea (perhaps down "rabbit holes" of interesting asides), readers expect continuity born of thorough composition and thoughtful revision. Tools such as research proposals, outlines, and topic threads prepare writers to enter a draft systematically, graciously, branch by branch.

The Christmas tree model may help writers visualize the shape of an argument, but developing a paragraph still takes practice and skill. Most writers have practiced these skills in conversation, but they need to transfer them to the page. Spoken conversations necessarily involve more than one person, which often leads to dynamic interchange and new ideas. When writers approach each branch of their argument as a possibility for vibrant exchange rather than as an evidence report, their writing becomes more vibrant. The topic thread frames this idea exchange, offering an opportunity to expand with an example or context. Contextualizing or offering an example particularizes a claim, promoting stronger empathy.

Though writers might be tempted to default to broader ideas or claims, especially in the shadow of a long assignment, specificity results in more comprehensive discussion and likelier connection with an audience. In this way, some of the same issues apply to draft development as to thesis development. Specificity often generates more explicit engagement and even, oddly enough, a more universal application than does a blanket, universal statement. We find good examples of this paradox in poetry; most good poems raise the universal through the specific, and the practice of poetry has much to offer any writer. Marie Howe's poem "Singularity," for instance, focuses on the impact of humans on the climate, but she never once references the looming idea of global warming. Instead, she writes about a time when creation was all so connected and knowingly interdependent that no one was "home alone / pulling open the drawer where the pills are kept."[1] Evoking these incredibly specific images of loneliness and disconnect helps her illustrate just how important it is to acknowledge and preserve interconnectedness. In an academic context, writers can apply these poetic lessons by engaging evidence to support specific claims and examples, making room for their own voices in response. Making knowledge active demands the work of synthesis, not simply summary and transition.

Constructive Conversations: Feedback and Conferencing

Once the draft is complete, time and distance can reveal lapses in topicality. Building rest time into the drafting process generates the objectivity and clarity needed to revisit the writing. Sometimes deadlines loom and writers rush their work, but part of my job as an instructor is to create small assignments along the way to encourage and facilitate some distance from the writing. Writers submit an introduction for feedback before they begin the entire draft, and by the time they are ready to submit a draft, they have had time to consider my response and their own relationship to the introduction. This small experience of time to consider their work encourages objectivity and demonstrates how effective reflection can be for the draft as a whole. Writers often have two weeks of time between rough draft submission and final draft submission in which we conduct peer reviews, individual conferences, and specific guided revision. As a side note, not long after I began using the conversational frame in composition teaching, I realized

1. Howe, "Singularity."

that my composition writers consistently submitted better work than my upper division English majors. The English majors are a talented group of students, often well-versed in good writing practices, but I had not created the same type of writing environment for them; instead, their traditional end-of-semester paper was due in the final week of class. Once I realized this discrepancy, I revised the writing process expectations for the English majors. Introducing smaller assignments, multiple draft requirements, and peer review significantly improved their work, and perhaps more importantly, it reframed the English assignment as a developing conversation rather than a final pronouncement on a text. Setting aside this time can feel luxurious or even frivolous, but it is essential to draft development and to the ongoing research conversation for all disciplines.

The time between rough draft and final submission creates essential space for listening—to one another, to the instructor, and to the draft itself. Peer review (as discussed extensively in chap. 3) initiates conversations about the draft that carry over to the individual conferences I conduct with each writer. Prior to each conference, I read and reflect on each draft, distilling my response into three or four overall observations (such as "strong prose" or "read aloud for continuity on page 2" or "strengthen topic claims throughout"). Throughout the draft, I will offer more specific feedback, including opportunities to improve clarity or development, as well as noting mechanical errors that could impede clarity or compromise ethos. Sometimes I ask questions in the margins or jot down a connection or source that might be helpful. Engaging with the draft prior to our conference facilitates more meaningful conversation with the writer, and though some of my suggestions will likely need to be taken as directives, not all of them will. The best part of a conference usually involves those places where a suggestion could be taken or not. When the writer arrives, I come around to the front of my desk, where we sit beside one another. If possible, I like to begin by asking how the writer feels about the draft. Then I offer my copy to the writer to hold. These small gestures emphasize my collaboration with the writer, and often help ease any anxieties about the feedback. Conferences are short, each one only five to seven minutes, yet they are powerful. Because we are both so familiar with the text, we can move quickly into substantive discussion. Though conferences often consume two or even three class periods, they provide crucial opportunities to connect with writers and for writers to ask important questions of themselves and their drafts.

Outside of a writing classroom, writers may not always have or take the necessary sustained time and space away from a draft before submission. One helpful technique to gain perspective that can quickly improve a draft is to read the draft aloud. Reading aloud allows us to inhabit the work in a new way. Often, if a sentence is unclear or if a paragraph strays from the topic, I ask the writer to read the section aloud to me. Invariably, writers sense almost immediately the confusion in the work. Reading aloud uses different parts of our brains, allowing us to process our own writing differently than we might in silent reading. I practice the read-aloud model in my own work too. Recently, as I was working on a book review presentation, reading aloud helped me reconsider transitions and even paragraph placement. What made perfect sense to me in the drafting process was clearly out of order when I read it aloud, and the practice helped me reorganize to guarantee my audience could follow my argument with ease.

After some time away from their drafts, writers return to the classroom and participate in a post-conference guided revision (appendix 5). Writers bring new drafts showcasing their responses to peer review and conferences, as well as any other revision progress they have made. Guided revision emphasizes reading aloud, either alone or to a partner, as well as other assigned revision tasks while I circulate for on-the-spot conferences where writers show me their revision progress or discuss problems. The enforced space between rough draft and final submission is not simply time off

from writing, but is instead filled with small, meaningful interactions with the draft. Guided revision acts as a sort of revision
laboratory where writers can experiment and test their work.

Tying Threads Together: Conclusions

If, as discussed in chapter 3, introductions help writers relate well
to their readers, the conclusion should help readers carry the topic
beyond the writing and into their communities. To conclude means,
of course, to end, but it also means "to draw a conclusion." The first
sense is more passive, and for many beginning writers, conclusions
are indeed passive. Approached passively, the conclusion func-
tions something like an appendix in the human body—a vestigial
reminder of something we could take or leave. After writing many
pages on a topic, writers may feel as if they have nothing left to
say, and they might willingly restate a thesis and list the points
they argued in the preceding pages. If writers instead approach
the conclusion as an opportunity to come to a new understanding,
however, it becomes more meaningful to writers and readers alike.
When I draw the Christmas tree model of writing, I do not place the
conclusion *on* the tree, but apart from it, a present to be savored
and unwrapped. I ask writers to imagine opening a present on
Christmas Day only to find something they already owned—their
favorite sweater simply dressed up with a bow, or even worse, a
bundle of lights, some branches, and a few ornaments. Imagining
the conclusion as a gift suggests that it should be at least a little
exciting—that it could be a thoughtful presentation of an essay's
arguments in more than just a colorful bow. The conclusion should
offer a takeaway, something to consider; it should put the research
in motion, raising questions or calling us to action.

Staying on topic does not mean boring repetition, and the conclusion is no exception. Topics, like conversations, are dynamic,
and I cannot think of a situation in which I would say to a friend,
"Thanks for talking with me. I discussed three points, and this was

my premise." The work of research, the work of making meaning, and the work of conversation changes us, and that growth can be reflected in the conclusion. Writing lore may suggest that writers should not "bring new ideas" to the conclusion, but what is a conclusion if not a new idea? Perhaps that dictum emerged from the wise advice not to add new argument branches to the conclusion, but over the years, that advice turned to a prohibition that gutted the spirit of the conclusion. Four questions can help writers draft and revise conclusions that say "aha!" instead of "the end":

- What did I learn/how did I grow in my understanding from this research?
- What do I want readers to carry with them into a broader conversation about this topic?
- What is at stake?
- What remains to be considered?

These questions can help, but conclusions are notoriously difficult. More than anything else we write, the conclusion benefits from some breathing room, perhaps because drawing conclusions involves that essential vulnerability of meaningful conversation. It takes time to discern exactly how the research conversation has impacted or changed us. I often advise writers simply to put down some roots, and to know that conclusions require time to germinate. Distilling research and logic into a concentrated understanding brings a topic to fruition, but it cannot be rushed. Even though conclusions are hard and first efforts are messy, it is often better to write even an ineffective conclusion and revise from there, because the process of being in dialogue with oneself can prompt the growth needed for a developed conclusion.

During the conclusion-writing process, writers might also find it helpful to isolate the introduction and read it against the conclusion. Introductions promise connection and direction to be cultivated and explored throughout the essay. The conclusion should demonstrate the growth that was promised in the introduction rather than simply repeat what the introduction previewed. Restating a thesis does not automatically indicate growth, but revisiting the *impact* of those thesis ideas might well indicate growth and also inspire more. The conclusion can offer a chance to return to an opening anecdote or bring a specific example full circle, providing a sense of closure as well as possibility. Putting the draft components in conversation can enrich the overall writing dialogue.

First Things Last: The Title

After completing the draft, writers can turn their attention to the title. Though the title may be a reader's first exposure to the work, it often only crystallizes near the end of the writing process. I encourage writers to keep a working title as they draft, but because an effective title distills the topic, it often needs revision once the draft is complete. Titles point the way into a draft, communicating not only the details of the essay but also the writer's voice. Academic titles can be all business or they can be playful, but they should always concisely convey the argument and scope of the essay. For example, the title "The Gender Gap in US Engineering" covers the topic and the regional scope of the essay, but it does not offer the scope of the argument itself. This perfunctory title sets up a report on the state of gender inequity in this field, and if it aims for a report, such a title would be fine. Consider, however, the revised title: "Bridging the Gender Gap in US Engineering." Here the writer alludes to an engineering marvel, the bridge, providing not only an insight into her actual proposal for change, but also into her wit.

Sometimes an academic title comes in two parts—the allusive or witty left side separated by a colon (or question mark) from the more perfunctory right side. The material on the right side is crucial, because it indicates what the paper is actually doing, but the left side often provides easier access to that work. Consider these two student titles:

"What Doesn't Kill You Makes You Stronger: Using Diseases to Treat Patients"

"Moore's Law or Moore's Flaw? Sustainability of an Industry Built on Exponential Growth"[2]

In the first example, the writer uses a familiar idiom to connect with readers and to contextualize his focus. In the second example, the rhyming play on words on the left softens and prefigures the lengthy, but necessary, description of the claim on the right. The witty part of a title generates interest and connection, and while it is not absolutely necessary, the effort required to make such a connection for readers indicates hospitality and goodwill.

To draft an effective title, writers can begin by listing three to five important key words or phrases from their work. These phrases should avoid abstractions such as "society" or "culture," focusing instead on specifics. Armed with these key words and phrases, the writer can place them in context, as in the engineering title, where the scope of the project looked only at US engineering data. Finally, the writer can look for connections and allusions. Of course, some disciplines, such as the sciences, often rely on an exciting discovery itself to generate that interest, or focus solely on methodology. Nevertheless, creating a title that reflects a writer's voice and claim as well as one that meets the reader's needs is a skill to be cultivated.

Staying on the Path: Being on Topic

Being on topic requires preparation, organization, and reflection, but at its heart, staying on topic is about being gracious, not about

2. Drake Shull, "What Doesn't Kill You Makes You Stronger: Using Diseases to Treat Patients," and Casey Williams, "Moore's Law or Moore's Flaw? Sustainability of an Industry Built on Exponential Growth," Composition 211: Sophomore Research Collection, Milligan University Digital Repository, https://mcstor.library.milligan.edu/handle/11558/4765, https://mcstor.library.milligan.edu/handle/11558/2858.

following a set of rules. The saying "interesting people are inter-ested" applies to the graciousness of being on topic. Writers who care about their work want others to care about it too, which means first choosing topics with intention. Once writers have invested deeply in a topic, everything from the research process to the orga-nization of the paper becomes an opportunity to involve others in the conversation, an opportunity to signal progress on the trail. The conversational framework emphasizes discovery and growth throughout the writing, offering signposts as writers navigate their own path through the research. Staying on topic allows both the reader and the writer to enter the forest confident that the path will lead them to a new understanding.

five

Be Engaging

In the wake of World War I, poets and writers of the mid-twentieth century mourned the loss of meaningful connections and of dynamic language to industrialization and globalism. Poets and authors such as T. S. Eliot, Gertrude Stein, and Ezra Pound criticized sparkling society conversation for being more glitter than substance, and they worked to reclaim the energy of language and cultivate meaningful connections. The drawing rooms where Eliot's J. Alfred Prufrock loiters while the society women "talk of Michelangelo" feel empty and meaningless because he is not engaged in the dialogue and the women have no desire to engage him.[1] At these parties, everyone participates in superficial, self-absorbed monologues aimed at no one in particular, society small talk of the highest degree. Prufrock's language and conversation fail to connect him to anyone. The problem of twentieth-century disengagement, one of increasing individualism and globalization, has only heightened in the twenty-first. To engage and be engaged includes risk and compromise, elements of conversation that require trust

1. Eliot, "Love Song of J. Alfred Prufrock," 4.

and practice. At its heart, being engaging is, of course, about being in relationship with others. The same ethical posture that brings us into respectful dialogue invites wit, authenticity, precision, and care with our language. Poor Prufrock was so busy putting on his society self and worrying about what he was expected to say that he failed to make authentic connections. Thankfully, Eliot's own commitment to poetic language—to imagery, etymology, phrasing, and allusion—suggests that not all is lost. We might think that being an engaging speaker or writer is simply a natural talent, something we are born with or not, but these kinds of skills can be learned and refined in dialogue with others, and particularly through the practice of poetry.

By practice of poetry, I mean the sort of engagement with others and with language that prioritizes imagination, immediacy, connectivity, and a wide scope of knowledge. Poet Denise Levertov describes her approach to poetry as "standing open-mouthed in the temple of life," which is to say, a posture of wonder, receptivity, and even uncertainty.[2] Poet Jane Hirshfield speaks of writing as a "ripening collaboration" of writer, audience, and the world, her recognition of writing as relationship.[3] Throughout poet Mary Oliver's work, but particularly in her collection of essays titled *Upstream*, she emphasizes the value and virtue of paying attention.[4] For Oliver, deep attention to a subject or a moment promotes an almost spiritual connection to the world around us, but that connection draws her into the life of other creatures. Indeed, "creature" and "creativity" share a word history, suggesting that the creative work of writing nurtures our creaturely imagination, connecting us ever more deeply to one another. Academic writing may seem the furthest genre from imagination or poetry, but writers can learn much from the practice of poetry, especially from its attention to form and transformation. Writing and reading poetry encourages

2. Levertov, "Some Notes on Organic Form," 421.
3. Hirshfield, *Ten Windows*, 4.
4. Oliver, "Upstream," 8.

the kind of engagement that elevates details and appreciates lyrical prose. Poets model how to engage ideas, how to cherish words, and how to slow down with language. Academic writing can and should convey information or argue a thesis, but engaging academic work can and should move and delight us as well.

Practice Attention: Getting Started

Paying attention, an important practice of poetry, encourages such delight. That is, even when we strive for simplicity and clarity, careful attention recognizes and realizes beauty in the ordinary. A traditional monastic practice, *lectio divina*, treats Scripture as a living conversation, as a practice in attention. In this practice, studying Scripture involves slow, careful reading, meditation, rest, and—only after all these steps—action. In many ways, it is not so different from the argument Heidegger makes for *logos*, or logic and speech, to include a sense of listening, shepherding, and gathering wisdom. Writers who practice *lectio divina* might read one passage or even one sentence while considering the impact and importance of each word or the relationship created by syntax or juxtaposition. Such careful attention to even a small passage can bring focus to an entire work.

For Mary Oliver, paying attention recognizes the web of mutuality involving us in the lives and stories of others and the world around us, leading to the kind of wonder we cannot help but share. Paying attention slows us down, a kind of *lectio divina* for living. Observations born of intentional and concentrated attention may go a long way toward elucidating a complex idea or collaborating with readers and evidence, even in academic writing. In her poem "Sometimes," Oliver's "instructions for living a life" include not only paying attention, but also wonder and testimony.[5] Paying attention, it turns out, helps us decenter ourselves from the

5. Oliver, "Sometimes," 37.

narrative, and often leads to having new and interesting things to say. When we couple attention with compassion and the willingness to be surprised, the result can be a posture of humility akin to that of engaged listening. Similar to Levertov's "open-mouthed" attitude, willingness to "be astonished" means readily admitting that we often do not yet know what we don't know.[6] And sharing the discoveries we make while attending to details and ordinary moments signals attention to community and relationships as well. In academic writing, it is easy to lose the wonder of astonishment, but writers who maintain their own astonishment motivate readers to do so as well. The practice of poetry transforms academic writing from an onerous, formula-driven task to a deliberate, potentially surprising interaction.

Necessary Trouble: Clarity

Engaging writing presents complex ideas simply and elegantly. Joseph Williams, in his book *Style: Lessons in Clarity and Grace*, traces the history of obscure and unclear writing from literature and history to science and medicine.[7] Sometimes trying to "sound smart," as we say in my classes, prevents clear presentation of the material, resulting in, at best, graceless prose, and at worst, a complete disconnect from readers and failure of argument. This past semester, a young man experienced this problem. In our spoken conversations, he was witty, engaged, and observant, but every time he put his pen to the page, his assumptions about what an academic audience might want from his prose stifled that voice. Once he embraced his own connection to the subject, his writing became more authentic, coherent, and cohesive. As Derek Thompson of *The Atlantic* notes, when writers feel insecure about their work they tend to resort to jargon. Notably, insecurity is often a failure of ethos, a lack of "good sense" resulting from insufficient

6. Oliver, "Sometimes," 37.
7. Williams and Bizup, *Style*, 3–6.

research on a topic. In my classes, we discuss how inflated rhetoric and jargon distance readers from writers, creating unnecessary barriers to the information. Thompson continues, "Complicated language and jargon offer writers the illusion of sophistication."[8] Contrary to the writing writers may have encountered in their own education, "academese" does not make a brilliant argument.

Trusty comic-book philosophers Calvin and Hobbes mock this academic propensity for obscure language. Calvin tells Hobbes: "I used to hate writing assignments, but now I enjoy them. I realized that the purpose of writing is to inflate weak ideas, obscure poor reasoning, and inhibit clarity. With a little practice, writing can be an intimidating and impenetrable fog!"[9] An "impenetrable fog" is the opposite of relatable. Too often it signals to readers that they are not educated enough to navigate the argument, when the failure actually belongs to the writer who refused to render complex topics simply and with clarity. The golden rule, "Treat others the way you would like to be treated," certainly applies to writing, and most readers want to access complex ideas without the language intruding. As so many writers and thinkers will attest, rendering complex ideas with simplicity and clarity requires far more work than pouring polysyllabic words onto the page.

Writers can avoid academese, as George Orwell says, by taking the "necessary trouble" to choose their words for themselves.[10] Orwell cared deeply about language because he saw how manipulating it could impoverish individual thought and the civic body. In his novel *1984*, a language called "newspeak" reduces all communication to confusing expediency. (The word itself is a combination of media and language—news and speak—in addition to a novel or new kind of language.) In his essay "Politics and the English Language," Orwell faults the media for perpetuating an assault

8. Derek Thompson, "Why Simple Is Smart," *Atlantic*, January 31, 2022, https://www.theatlantic.com/ideas/archive/2022/01/writing-tips-for-journalists-jargon-simplicity/621411.

9. Watterson, *Homicidal Psycho Jungle Cat*, 62.

10. Orwell, "Politics and the English Language," 355.

on language, but he also faults scholars who perpetuate what he considers an unscrupulous style of exclusive, jargon-filled, and abstracted language. He posits several questions a writer can ask to avoid these pitfalls, including "What am I trying to say?" and "Have I said anything that is avoidably ugly?"[11] A writer must confront weak ideas that need to be reworked or discarded, while considering how to promote instead of inhibit clarity. Asking "What am I trying to say?" prevents a writer (one would hope) from saying things that are "avoidably ugly." Certainly, it would be easier to use ready-made phrases or imitate academic jargon, but respect for language and for readers makes the trouble of tempering complexity with clarity not just necessary but worthwhile.

Every year at least a few of my students who complete their self-evaluations indicate that they would like to work on increasing their vocabularies. Of course, a larger vocabulary offers more possibilities, but I always advocate not for a wider vocabulary, but for a deeper one. Simplicity does not mitigate creativity or musicality, and though it might mean choosing smaller words, it still requires sensitivity to a word's history and etymology. Having a sense of a word's impact or history can change the nuance of an argument, both as it is made and received. Both fiction and poetry can point academic writers to the potential of a perfect word. Twentieth-century poet Ezra Pound founded a whole movement, Imagism, on finding the perfect words to evoke an experience. He revised his poem "In the Station of the Metro" from thirty-one lines to just two, meaning that every word performed an important function:

> The apparition of these faces in the crowd;
> Petals on a wet, black bough.[12]

Students often notice that "bough" could be "branch," but that the experience of the poem changes with the harder "*ch*" sound

11. Orwell, "Politics and the English Language," 362.
12. Pound, "In the Station of the Metro," 111.

instead of the softer *"ough"* at the end echoing the ephemeral, yet remarkable quality of the vision itself. Exchanging any of the words might change either the meaning or the impact of the poem, just as a specific word choice in an essay might emphasize or detract from a claim (consider the difference between "angry" and "mad," for instance). Even the simplest words can bring precision and depth in the breadth of their history, etymology, connotation, and denotation. Of course, at least one clever student of mine has asked if our own assignment could be reduced from thirty-five hundred words to fourteen in the spirit of Poundian simplicity, which I have had to decline. Though researched and sustained arguments require a few more than two lines, they do still benefit from a similar precise and thoughtful approach to language.

Fiction writers also offer important lessons about a careful, poetic approach to language. Margaret Atwood's *Oryx and Crake* charts the ecological and cultural disintegration of a civilization much like ours. In her novel, the main character, Snowman, recalls all the abuses to language that prevented clear and meaningful communication. At the end of the novel, he witnesses what is likely his final sunrise, remarking that he "gazes at it with rapture; there is no other word for it. *Rapture.* The heart seized, carried away, as if by some large bird of prey."[13] Though the novel itself has traced the consequences of language neglected, like Eliot, Atwood gestures toward the importance of tending language carefully. Atwood's novel has good company among apocalyptic novels that emphasize the importance of language. Cormac McCarthy's *The Road* features a father and son moving slowly toward the coast following some unnamed destructive event. As their world has diminished, so has their language: "The world shrinking down about a raw core of parsible entities. The names of things slowly following those things into oblivion. Colors. The names of birds. Things to eat. Finally the names of things one believed to be true. More fragile than he would

13. Atwood, *Oryx and Crake*, 371.

have thought."[14] Perhaps dystopian writers care so much about precise diction because they see the connection between precise language and the integrity necessary to live in harmony. Author Rebecca Solnit observes that when writers strive for linguistic integrity, it creates "a kind of wholeness and connectedness, between language and what it describes, between one person and another, or between members of a community or society."[15] Writers, even and especially writers of academic research, bear the responsibility for the words they choose and the impact those words might have. Perhaps academic writers bear even more responsibility to approach words with care, given that so many academic publications yield to exclusive, jargon-oriented language. Marilyn Chandler McEntyre writes, "Everyone who writes with care, who treats words with tenderness and allows even the humblest its historical and grammatical dignity, participates in the exhilarating work of reclamation."[16] Writers such as Eliot, Atwood, and McCarthy caution us not to abandon our responsibility to linguistic integrity, and a practice of poetry invites all writers, not just poets and authors, into this exhilarating work.

Words in Relationship: Syntax

Choosing words carefully also means thinking about sentence architecture, the combination of syntax and diction. Virginia Tufte, in her lovely and useful text *Artful Sentences: Syntax as Style*, writes that syntax "gives words the power to relate to one another in a sequence."[17] Engaging writing takes place on this molecular level where words juxtaposed with other words create new meaning simply by their placement or cooperation. For example, Orwell writes that "the decadence of our language is

14. McCarthy, *The Road*, 88–89.
15. Solnit, *Orwell's Roses*, 232.
16. McEntyre, *Word Tastings*, viii.
17. Tufte, *Artful Sentences*, 9.

probably curable."[18] Placing the word "probably" in front of "curable" lends uncertainty, hope, and urgency to the sentence; that word "probably" implies we ought to keep reading to find out how and why a cure is not assured. Mindful syntax considers the power of words in relationship.

Any number of style guides will offer advice about how to write clear prose, and I do not intend to replicate that kind of work here. When I encounter poorly constructed sentences, however, they usually fail to consider the way words relate to one another, particularly in verb choice, prepositions, and nominalizations (a noun created from a verb form). Like Orwell, I support active verbs, in part because they tighten the relationship between the subject and the predicate. Consider this sentence from a first draft:

> Many Americans are prevented from engaging with their full range of freedoms.

The key to the sentence is the prevention, but by whom? Rather than state a claim or enter the conversation more emphatically, the writer makes a more passive observation. This type of sentence, while it reads well and has an "academic" sound, says less than it might. Consider the revised version:

> Racist and classist policies exclude many Americans from freedoms enjoyed by a wealthy, White majority.

In this version, the writer committed to a stronger, more specific argument. Even the verb changed, from a less intense and passive "are prevented" to a more intentional and active "exclude." The writing that follows from this sentence will require more of the writer in terms of research and dialogue, but it is also more likely to contribute to the conversation more specifically and meaningfully.

18. Orwell, "Politics and the English Language," 364.

Passive voice verbs, often maligned, do have a place in clear writing, particularly if the writing is scientific or if they want to emphasize the action rather than the actor. In the first sentence, however, the passive voice does not lend power or clarity to the sentence, and it limits the sentence's impact. Syntax offers many options for building sentences, enough to be overwhelming at times, but having a clear sense of what we want to say and a desire to avoid ugliness can help us navigate those choices.

In topic claims and threads especially, a strong verb directs and elevates the argument. Too often (though not always) a linking verb or a "being verb" (am, is, are, was, were) breaks no new ground for the claim. Consider this sentence:

> The policies preventing many Americans from engaging with freedom are problematic.

Here, the linking verb sets up a grammatical construction called a predicate adjective. Compared to the earlier sentence, this one sets up a summary of policy problems rather than the impact of those problems. Depending on the goal of the paragraph, summary might be needed, but writing that consists entirely of summative paragraphs shies away from the kind of engagement needed for deeper dialogue. Being verbs have their place, and they certainly do a lot of heavy lifting for writers. Indeed, Orwell's claim that "the decadence of our language *is* probably curable" occupies the first sentence of a new paragraph, followed by robust discussion of his point. Though by no means do I suggest eliminating all being verbs, sometimes it is constructive to simply ask "What does this subject *do* besides exist?" Especially when asked about a topic claim, this step can help writers—particularly beginning writers—frame the thought, and consequently the paragraph, more substantively.

Weaker verbs often force syntax into unwieldy construction and make for "avoidably ugly" sentences. Two symptoms of weaker verbs include nominalizations and preposition overload. Consider this sentence:

> The exclusion of many Americans from basic freedoms is a result of racist and classist policies.

In this sentence, the earlier version's "exclude" becomes a noun, "exclusion," forcing the sentence toward a linking verb with a predicate nominative ("result" renames "exclusion"). Though the sentence still conveys much of the same information, it loses clarity of argument and adds a third prepositional phrase—meaning that it says less while using more words.

Prepositional phrases and prepositions help connect and relate nouns to actions and to other nouns, but too many prepositions often introduce distance that strains the relationship. Consider the sentence:

> Policies prevent Americans in lower socio-economic and minority groups from the fruits of America's guarantee of freedom for all.

Here, concatenated prepositional phrases (or preposition trains, as they are often called) considerably delay the meaning and impact of the verb "prevent." Being more intentional about preposition usage can help writers be more intentional in relating their ideas to readers overall.

Reading for these syntax symptoms during the revision process can improve not only the sentence-level architecture, but the structure of the broader argument. Wendell Berry writes in his essay "Standing by Words" that "a sentence that is completely shapeless is therefore a loss of thought, an act of self-abandonment to incoherence."[19] For all writers, but especially beginning writers, considering syntax embodies the work of thinking, of articulating self and engaging with others.

19. Berry, *Standing by Words*, 53–54.

Cleaning the Closet: First Efforts

As writers prepare to enter a conversation, they must necessarily consider their research. Engaging writers take every opportunity to engage with the research itself, from the proposal and the annotated bibliography to the draft itself. In the least engaging writing, evidence dots the landscape, more as a gesture toward a requirement than as true dialogue. In contrast, writers who respond vigorously, dynamically, and compassionately to other writers, data, and statistics create space for more and more interesting conversation. Steps such as the annotated bibliography introduce writers to potential interactions, but instructors can support this type of connection throughout the writing process. One early activity includes a journal article evaluation, in which writers must summarize the article and evaluate its presentation (Is it a strong model of academic clarity and accessibility? Is it timely and relevant?). Most importantly, they must devote an entire section of the review to their response to the argument. Writers might use the response section to rebut the argument using other research, make a connection to a contemporary event or personal experience, respond to the practicality of the argument, or consider instead how to build from the argument. The response presents writers with an initial opportunity to engage the research as more than a gesture toward requirements.

Another helpful activity includes the "three-minute application." The amount of time is not terribly important, but through trial and error, three minutes seems to work well for most students. Unlike the journal review and the annotated bibliography, which should take place before the writer begins drafting, this activity can happen anytime. It can be particularly helpful midway through the drafting process when writers begin to flag. Writers choose any piece of evidence they plan to use and conduct a sustained reading of it for three minutes in *lectio divina* style. After three minutes of thoughtful consideration, students respond in writing to the evidence for three minutes more. This activity, grounded in the practice of poetry, asks writers to slow their interaction, to approach not just their writing, but also their reading and listening, with intention and care.

Beginning a draft follows those initial steps of proposal and research, of sitting with the outline and the evidence and listening to the conversations in progress. After all this preparation and thinking, diving into the draft might feel momentous and even paralyzing. My husband, a skilled physician and communicator, complains that sitting down to write often results in a prose and a voice that does not feel authentic to him. Yet when he speaks, he makes reasoned, clever connections and often elucidates complex problems clearly and succinctly. In part, he struggles with his expectations of writing to be somehow more formal, and in part, he overthinks his approach to the material. His experience reflects that of many writers for whom a mute blank screen or a garbled sentence seems all the more puzzling because speaking about a topic comes easily to them. Writing multiple drafts can help writers find an authentic voice.

The way writers draft also impacts their writing voice. Looking at a blank screen and watching the word count tick slowly upward (or in the worst case, remain resolutely at zero) can discourage even the most stalwart and accomplished writer. Many writers expect to open their laptops and crank out an essay on the first try, but writing rarely proves to be that straightforward. Many high schools expect students to complete their work through learning management software, meaning that many students learn to draft on their computers only. To ease students into a draft, I often invite them to begin by drafting with pen and paper. My own son, a good writer and strong student, struggled to organize and develop his thoughts on his computer. Drafting by hand helped him clarify his thinking, and then typing his written work into the software system acted as a first revision. Several recent studies indicate that handwriting engages the brain more completely than typing, and by encouraging students to undertake the first drafting steps on paper, I hope to help them process their ideas more successfully, as my son experienced.[20] Compared to the permanence of a deleted phrase on a computer, sometimes simply seeing the progress of crossed-out words or stops and starts can be encouraging.

It might be daunting to think about choosing the perfect words or constructing artful sentences, because conveying an idea clearly can be difficult enough. For that reason, many of these style skills come from repetition and familiarity with writing. Such familiarity means multiple drafts, lower-stakes assignments with timely feedback, opportunities for thoughtful revision, and engagement with models of effective, ethically postured writers. Yet even the most experienced writers would agree that most sentence-level craft takes place in revision. I often tell my students to go ahead and "write it ugly," if that helps get the idea to the page. Revision allows for reflection on word choice and syntax that might inhibit the drafting process. For too many writers, the first draft has historically become the final draft. Writing only one draft prevents writers from engaging with themselves, a necessary step in engaging with others. But spending time drafting without the expectation of permanence frees writers to be more authentic. Anne Lamott gives writers permission to write "shitty first drafts," a more colorful way of saying "write it ugly." She says that "almost all good writing begins with terrible first efforts."[21]

Returning to a draft feels like sifting through my closet. How did some of these pieces stay here so long? What was I thinking when I purchased this hideous blouse? Or, wait—these two pieces fit nicely together. I do not need those shoes, but I will never part with this particularly elegant scarf. The freedom to write messy drafts that will inevitably require revision makes room for authenticity, not perhaps on the first try, but as we continue to understand what works for us.

20. Askvik, van der Weel, and van der Meer, "Importance of Cursive Handwriting Over Typewriting," 2.
21. Lamott, *Bird by Bird*, 25.

The Three T's: Writing the Draft

Writing requires full concentration, and writing conducted in fits and starts will likely lack continuity and elegance of argument. While drafting is a messy, individual process, if writers approach it without care, the draft will present far fewer salvageable passages. Even with permission to write it ugly, engaged drafting still requires what I call "the three T's": time, total concentration, and a "trail of crumbs." Every writer needs a chunk of time to focus and sustain a thought, but it need not be a whole day or even an entire hour. If a writer can eliminate distractions, even a short amount of time can be productive, but total concentration can be difficult to manage. Brain research indicates that interruptions do more damage to our thought process and momentum than we might imagine.[22] Interruptions such as email or text notifications, even a silenced buzz, can break the nascent synapse in our brains. Writing on a computer exacerbates the interruptions and temptation to stray from the task. Committing to a writing project means turning off devices and organizing a distraction-free period. I tell students to set a timer and not to move away from their writing—even if it feels unproductive—until the timer chimes. Dealing with emails and text messages as they come in gives the illusion of productivity, but it leaves little room for concentration. Engaging writing begins as a contract between the writer and the task at hand.

As writers draft this way over the course of many days, I suggest also a trail of crumbs. Sophie Leroy, a specialist in organizational science, suggests in her work on attention that we often overestimate how much we will remember from one day to the next; she recommends making a "ready to resume plan" that can help us focus and pick up where we left off.[23] Anyone who writes vocationally can attest to the benefits of such a process. Outlines can help

22. Leroy, "Why Is It So Hard to Do My Work?," 168–81.
23. Peter Kelley, "Task Interrupted: A Plan for Returning That Helps You Move On," University of Washington News, January 16, 2018, https://www.washington.edu/news/2018/01/16/task-interrupted-a-plan-for-returning-helps-you-move-on.

point the draft in the right direction, but daily writing often leads to new revelations, to standing "open-mouthed" in the wake of new insights. A trail of crumbs leads a writer back to the concentration and focus of the previous day. It can be as simple as a short list, a phrase, or a new topic thread yet to be explored, but sometimes simply having words at the top of the page can relieve the anxiety of starting fresh. Writer's block can and does happen, but good preparation combined with time, concentration, and a marked path can see a writer through.

Practicing Poetry: Ethics of Engagement

The practice of poetry, while it certainly emphasizes the beauty of language and the art of attention, also sits honestly with the tension of uncertainty. Levertov enters the temple of life open-mouthed not because she knows what is to come but precisely because she does not. Hirshfield writes that "to be human is to be unsure," and that writing that "deepens the humanness in us" will likely tolerate some amount of uncertainty as well.[24] For academic writers, engaging with uncertainty means acknowledging anomalies or outliers in the research. Wrestling with contradiction honestly and transparently offers more to readers than a too-easy solution or a perfectly supported argument. Accommodating uncertainty also means being willing to have a partial answer but not a definitive one. It may mean posing more questions or calling for conversation, but it is not the same as unfinished or incomplete research. Uncertainty born from careful research and consideration recognizes limits and can lead to new conversations.

Being engaging means being in relationship. From the moment we turn toward a topic, we collaborate with other scholars who precede us, with our surroundings and experiences, with our readers, and with language itself. The first law of ecology is that everything

---

24. Hirshfield, *Ten Windows*, 149.

is connected to everything else. In the writing ecosystem, even the tiniest word choice influences engagement. Rebecca Solnit writes that "each word is a set of relationships, direct and indirect, a species in an ecosystem."[25] Language frames our interaction with the world around us as well as our response to it. Writing gives us the space and time to consider carefully how we want to do the important work of responding.

Many less-than-ethical approaches to engaging writing exist—incendiary language, egregious fallacies, an overreliance on pathos. It is certainly possible to engage an audience through fear or manipulated data, but those approaches do not respect the civic body, nor do they value legitimate discourse. An ethics of engagement aligns with the ethics of curiosity, listening, and open-mindedness that promote growth and change. Perhaps more importantly, an ethics of engagement recognizes thinking as a process. Rodin's famous sculpture *The Thinker* at first seems to support the idea of an individual pondering powerful questions alone. But Rodin's *Thinker* emerged from the clay only with the help of the artist, who in turn was deep in conversation with his artistic community, particularly Michelangelo, and with Dante's *Inferno*, which inspired the work. Many art scholars have connected the nudity of *The Thinker* to Dante's contemplation of suffering; yet the nudity could also suggest the transparency and vulnerability involved in thinking, and his receptive posture, bent forward chin to hand, might also indicate he is listening and waiting to "be astonished."[26] *The Thinker*, originally and aptly titled *The Poet*, embodies this contemplative poetic practice, bringing the sculpture (and by extension, Rodin and his community) into conversation with thousands of viewers who experience the piece every day. So much of our daily interaction, cluttered with input and often focused on expediency, precludes the practice of poetry. Corrosive and combative conversation exists and will continue to

25. Solnit, *Orwell's Roses*, 229.
26. Oliver, "Sometimes."

exist, but ethical engagement offers writers an alternative. Writing in and for a community is a practice of curiosity, generosity, and ultimately, hope. When we enter our writing hopeful for change, even and especially within ourselves, *how* we say becomes just as important as *what* we say.

six

Be Open-Minded

The *Oxford English Dictionary* attributes the first use of the term "open-minded" to Samuel Richardson's eighteenth-century novel *Clarissa*. Richardson writes that for some people, "all the world should be open-minded but themselves."[1] Richardson encapsulates the problem of being open-minded: we often think we are more open-minded than we really are. Pepperdine researchers Elizabeth Krumrei-Mancuso and Stephen Rouse confirm our overestimation of what they call "intellectual humility," or open-mindedness.[2] Krumrei-Mancuso and Rouse define intellectual humility as "accepting that one's knowledge and cognitive faculties are limited and imperfect."[3] In a culture where being right carries so much consequence and where admitting ignorance or changing opinions often signals weakness, intellectual humility can be in short supply. Cultivating intellectual humility, or open-mindedness, promotes

1. *Oxford English Dictionary* online (subscription required), s.v. "open-minded (adj.)," accessed March 2022, https://www.oed.com/view/Entry/259299.
2. Krumrei-Mancuso and Rouse, "Comprehensive Intellectual Humility Scale," 214–15.
3. Krumrei-Mancuso and Rouse, "Comprehensive Intellectual Humility Scale," 209.

"collaboration and civil discourse," which we need more than ever.[4] The Pepperdine research offers a helpful framework for writing, one that privileges "concern for knowledge and truth" over and above intellectual status or preconceptions.[5] Krumrei-Mancuso and Rouse identify four measurable qualities that help nurture intellectual humility:[6]

- respect for other viewpoints
- lack of intellectual arrogance
- ability to separate ego from intellect
- willingness to revise

Nurturing an ethical approach to the writing conversation, and in this case the particularly ethical virtue of open-mindedness, presupposes ethical motivations in writing. Intellectually humble writers begin projects knowing that they have something to learn. The writing classroom offers an opportunity to develop open-mindedness in shared dialogue and community with other writers.

Best Insights: Intellectual Humility

Intellectual humility begins in deep listening and compassion for other viewpoints. Christian ethicist Ellen Ott Marshall writes extensively about how to communicate well even in spaces and times of conflict. She recommends listening for a person's "best insights" rather than the "weakest argument," and seeking "common concerns and shared hopes."[7] Notably, effective instructors also listen for "best insights" in each writer's work, helping writers to discern their most promising lines of inquiry. Most instructors

4. Krumrei-Mancuso and Rouse, "Comprehensive Intellectual Humility Scale," 209.
5. Krumrei-Mancuso and Rouse, "Comprehensive Intellectual Humility Scale," 209.
6. Krumrei-Mancuso and Rouse, "Comprehensive Intellectual Humility Scale," 215.
7. Marshall, *Introduction to Christian Ethics*, 149.

would agree that offering positive feedback in conjunction with critical feedback promotes better revision, but listening for best insights requires more than just positive feedback; it requires specific, substantive comments about the writer's potential. I will always remember the generosity of a professor who, after listening to me talk about my wide-ranging ideas for a master's thesis, helped me sift my best insights from the chaff. My mind was cluttered with competing ideas and research, but he could see my best ideas more clearly than I could, and by pointing me toward them, he helped me clarify my thinking. That kind of listening for best insights is particularly valuable, but it is not as difficult as listening generously to someone with whom we completely disagree. In conversation, disagreements can often escalate into arguments where we wait to talk instead of listening openly. Approaching differing viewpoints with a posture of humility "requires discipline to create in ourselves space to receive" views with which we disagree.[8] Even considering opposing ideas can feel threatening, but according to Krumrei-Mancuso and Rouse, "being intellectually humble does not mean that one blindly adopts the views of others or lacks confidence in one's own beliefs and values."[9] It is possible, then, to make space for conflicting viewpoints without compromising personal beliefs, to remain confident even while engaging in listening that might change our minds. Writers have the advantage of time and space to practice listening with generosity instead of skepticism.

Weighing Bananas: Respecting Different Viewpoints

Like any discipline, making space requires intention and practice. Outside the classroom, travel helps reorient perspectives. While traveling in Europe, I discovered how different the grocery-shopping experience could be when I tried to check out without

8. Marshall, *Introduction to Christian Ethics*, 149.
9. Krumrei-Mancuso and Rouse, "Comprehensive Intellectual Humility Scale," 220.

first weighing my bananas. With the line backing up behind me, I began to sweat as the other customers eyed me impatiently while the cashier gestured (neither of us speaking the other's language) toward the scale outside. Perhaps she saw me as an ignorant American tourist, but nevertheless, she stepped away from her counter, guided me through the process, and accepted my profuse apology. I carry that memorable, if seemingly insignificant, encounter with me whenever I travel as a reminder that my way of doing things is not the only or right way. Travel to other countries and experiencing another culture can certainly shift our presumptions about the world, but even a short excursion can help. Driving to a big city from a small one, attending a different denomination or faith congregation for worship, or even trying a different cuisine can shake loose some of our biases. Each weekend my family and I try to cook a new-to-us ethnic cuisine. On one occasion, my daughter predicted she would not like the dish, but she was so pleasantly surprised that she requested we have it again. She was practicing an openness and cognitive flexibility that allowed her to taste the dish *and* admit she liked it despite her earlier prediction. This attitude can enhance experience and communication of all types, especially writing. Some of my favorite student writing projects are the ones that lead to unexpected conclusions, because in those projects, the writers learn more about the world and themselves.

Novels and documentaries can also open us to new perspectives, offering a sort of "armchair travel." Deliberately choosing stories of other cultures or experiences can strengthen our ability to hold space for difference. Though I teach about the Vietnam War every spring, it was Viet Thanh Ngyuen's novel *The Sympathizer* that opened the intimate brutalities and complexities of the war to me. Ngyuen's fictional account of a North Vietnamese spy working as an aide to a South Vietnamese general explores the narrator's and the country's divided sense of self, and it offers a completely different experience of American and French involvement. Because of

Ngyuen's novel, born of his own history, I can approach that period with more nuance and understanding.

Though not everyone has time or resources to travel or read widely, we can control how we consume media. The more we engage with social media, the more algorithms determine our content and show us more of what we want to hear. As early as 2011, Eli Pariser coined the term "filter bubble" to describe the impact of algorithms on information consumption.[10] As media fragments into specialized offerings—and as specialized social media options, in particular, increase—researchers are working to discern the impact on users. Meanwhile, we would be wise to reflect carefully on our information sources. Even without algorithms, it is easy to gravitate toward information that affirms our assumptions and biases. We might even feel like we are doing a good job of being informed, when in fact we are simply choosing comfortable material. Online options offer greater access to information than ever before, but to paraphrase the immortal words of Uncle Ben to Spiderman Peter Parker, with great access to information comes great responsibility. Purposefully spending time with alternative viewpoints by understanding media bias and intentionally cultivating a diverse newsfeed can help broaden our algorithm and increase our ability to sit with new or opposing viewpoints.

The writing classroom can foster respect for other viewpoints by encouraging open-ended questions and deep listening, as covered in chapters 1 and 2. Writers can also follow Ellen Ott Marshall's advice to listen for best insights by evaluating:

- What can I learn from this person?
- Where do our concerns align?
- What is the best insight of this argument?
- What question can I ask to open the dialogue instead of shutting it down?[11]

10. Pariser, *Filter Bubble*.
11. Marshall, *Introduction to Christian Ethics*, 149–50.

Activities such as the counterargument summary (see chap. 2) or the annotated bibliography (appendix 3) provide opportunities to consider these questions, but one of the most overlooked resources is time. Too often, writers rush to quick judgment and seek out research that confirms their position. Considering another viewpoint thoughtfully requires more time than we often allot for research and writing, but building in time to reflect, review, and revise creates space to acknowledge what we do not know. Being open-minded prompts us to ask another question instead of rushing to respond.

Don't Take It Personally: Ego and Intellect

Cultivating respect for other viewpoints also demands that we give up intellectual arrogance and sever the link between ego and intellect. Separating ego from intellect means that we do not equate our personal worth with positive reception of our ideas and beliefs. That is, if a person contradicts our belief or ideas, we can engage without feeling personally attacked or belittled. Cultivating this characteristic could be especially useful in contemporary discourse in which heightened emotions and identity politics threaten to stall conversations before they begin. Zen master Thich Nhat Hanh understands the ability to entertain alternative viewpoints dispassionately as "mindfulness of compassion."[12] For Hanh, treating an opposing viewpoint with compassion requires deliberate openness, which he sees as a generative and active process for both participants.

Open-mindedness promotes a sort of conversational hospitality that recognizes our potential to occupy roles as guest and host, sometimes in need of hospitality, sometimes dispensing it. The work of compassion not only invites us to see another's point of view, but it also invites us to evaluate our own belief through their

12. Hanh, *Art of Communicating*, 43.

eyes. What might seem eminently logical and essential to us might be threatening to someone else. Evaluating emotional reactions to dissonance might involve asking:

- Why do I feel threatened by this view or this response to my view?
- What can I learn from this criticism?
- Does my reaction reveal a blind spot in my thinking?
- What questions can I ask that will help me understand this view more completely?
- How could I separate my personal worth from my belief?

The last question in particular invites writers to see criticism and opposition not as a personal attack, but as an invitation to think critically and understand more deeply. Separating ego from intellect through compassion can build relationship and understanding of others and ourselves.

When we conflate our beliefs or knowledge with our value, we risk becoming intellectually rigid and arrogant. Even experts can learn from those with different experiences and perspectives. Fresh out of college and long before my graduate studies, I began teaching English in a New Hampshire high school. Though I was nominally the expert in the room, when a student asked why some comparative constructions receive the suffix *-er* and some use "more," I did not know. In my own speech and writing, I make those adjustments instinctively because of my lifelong immersion in my primary language. When a foreign exchange student raised her hand to interject that the decision depends on a word's syllables, it was a little embarrassing that she knew the answer when I did not, but the students were gracious, and we all learned something that day. The students did not expect me to know everything, and that moment of my ignorance sparked a sense of mutuality in the classroom. The exchange student's expertise in English grammar outstripped my own because of the way she had engaged it through study and dissection, while I had a blind spot for something I had intuited. That was the first of many times I would have to admit I did not know something or that I was wrong, but in the classroom, as in life, not knowing offers an opportunity for discovery. Sometimes familiarity, and even education, can create blind spots. Intellectual humility can keep learning fresh and new. Leaving behind intellectual arrogance means recognizing that we cannot know everything and that we can be enriched by one another.

Seeing Again: Willingness to Revise

Revising our ideas and our work is a key component of open-minded intellectual humility, which begins with a willingness to change and leads to a stronger sense of what is important. For philosopher Simone Weil, this humility is "a far more precious treasure than all academic progress."[13] Weil believes that reflecting on our faults "attentively and slowly" yields more progress than simply arriving at answers or completing tasks.[14] Willingness to revise involves willingly accepting criticism, admitting what we don't know, and taking care to involve other voices in our work. Writers have multiple opportunities to practice revision throughout the process, whether in the research stage or in the writing stage. Sometimes the evidence alone convinces writers to revise a claim. One semester a writer wanted to explore the threats of increased teen pregnancy only to find that teen pregnancy rates were actually declining. Faced with these facts, she began evaluating why she held those beliefs, revising and rethinking along the way. She began asking new questions of the evidence, and instead of proceeding as if she had the answer to be proven, she was more willing to listen and let her opinion evolve.

Ralph Waldo Emerson wrote, "A foolish consistency is the hobgoblin of little minds."[15] He probably intended the "little" of his

13. Weil, "Right Use of School Studies," 109.
14. Weil, "Right Use of School Studies," 109.
15. Emerson, "Self-Reliance," 133.

observation as an admonition against close-minded thinking, but the size strikes me as important. In terms of actual physicality, a foolish consistency does not need much room; it invites no guests, it brooks no dialogue. A foolish consistency provides the safety and security of a small, enclosed space, which by another interpretation might be called a prison. Clinging to long-held beliefs simply because they are long-held acts as a sort of armor, and though armor might feel protective, it still confines and restricts. It also prevents much in the way of connection and community. Revising an old opinion can be frightening, but divorcing intellect from ego and engaging intellectual humility provides far better protection from the hobgoblins.

Though the research process provides ample opportunities to revise one's thinking and approach, most writers associate revision with draft work. Drafting itself involves the give-and-take of vision and revision. I enjoy the visual, visceral process of writing longhand that bears out the false starts and progress on the page, chronicling my conversation with myself and the material along the way. Others prefer the cleaner lines of word processing and the permanence of the delete button. Even though most writers participate in major revision after completing the draft, revision is a constant process. Effective full-draft revision requires that writers commit to:

- separating effort from quality
- conducting macro and micro revisions
- revising as part of an ongoing conversation

Writers in my classes often observe that revision is both maddening and gratifying, and that more time spent in preparation, such as research and drafting, tips the scales toward gratifying.

When we hold tightly to the effort involved in writing, it can be hard to hear criticism. Effort spent writing does not always equal the result we might desire. I could spend many hours composing a symphony, but without training and experience, my piece will likely need significant revision. However beautiful the melody in my head, it may not translate to the page. To bring forward my melody and to render it playable by musicians, I need to study other effective works, prepare, practice, and of course, revise. Writers whose preliminary work includes seeking out strong models of good writing and working purposefully through the proposal and research process can improve their end results. The *type* of effort we give to a task, particularly writing, also matters. Weil writes that "twenty minutes of concentrated untired attention is infinitely better than three hours of the kind of frowning application that leads to a [false sense of] duty done."[16] Of course, she also notes that this effort is "much more difficult."[17] Sitting at the computer for hours without preparation can feel like "duty done" but it may not amount to much. For Weil, concentrated, prepared effort blossoms out of the "joy of learning," and while not every assignment may feel like joy, reframing it as an opportunity to learn changes the tenor of commitment to the task.[18] Revision cannot be the fail-safe for a draft written without preparation.

The type of effort we give to revision also matters, and it involves both micro and macro revisions. Macro revisions attend to organization and readability. When a writer struggles with macro revision, I often recommend the boringly named "highlighter revision" to trace the flow of ideas. The writer first identifies major focal ideas of the claim and assigns a color to each of those ideas. We then move through the draft together, highlighting each idea as it appears. Often, the exercise results in multicolored paragraphs that show clearly where the draft falters in focus and development. This process helps writers visualize the potential confusion as well as the potential reorganization of the draft, often with much success. Not every writer will need such intense macro revisions, but

16. Weil, "Right Use of School Studies," 111.
17. Weil, "Right Use of School Studies," 111.
18. Weil, "Right Use of School Studies," 110.

when and if they do, an instructor who can "listen for best insights" can often help redirect a draft with good results.

At the other end of the spectrum, micro revision is sometimes cast as "editing" in which writers dash off a draft, review it for spelling errors, and then consider it finished. While editing is important, micro revisions can also attend to many details of elegance, including word choice, syntax, and transitions. Like a host preparing the final details of a meal, writers focus on word work to improve ethos and clarity, making the entire experience of reading their writing more pleasurable.

Writers need to think of draft revision as an ongoing conversation, one that begins in research and continues even after final submission. Writers need due dates, not as looming threats, but because revision really could go on forever. Indeed, many writers could attest to finding potential revisions even in published work. Mary Shelley famously revised *Frankenstein* in 1831 after it had already been published in 1818. Her revisions reflected her ongoing conversation with the characters and with herself. Having suffered loss and grief, she revised the novel to reflect her new understanding of the world. Andreas Vesalius, often regarded as the father of modern anatomy, notoriously took to his margins to annotate his 1543 publication *De humani corporis fabrica* (*The Fabric of the Human Body*). Despite the enormous undertaking of printing and publication in the sixteenth century, he marked errors and recast sentences for elegance at every stage—before, during, and after binding. As he continued to learn more about human anatomy, he wanted his text to reflect his new understanding, but importantly, he also wanted his writing to convey that knowledge as clearly as possible. The potential for growth and new learning is one major reason why I discourage students from recycling old work completed for other classes. At the very least, when we re-engage with our old work, we can revisit the research, but more than likely, our own growth will demand significant revision of that work. We need a balance between revising forever and not at all.

To that end, writers need models of strong revision and opportunities to practice revising in and out of class, including conferences,
in-class guided revision, post-draft revision, and self-directed days
dedicated solely to revision.

Post-draft revision can be overwhelming, especially given the
pace of a collegiate writing course. To help manage the sometimes
unwieldy revision process, I offer a discrete revision assignment
called the revision workshop designed to help writers apply specific feedback (appendix 6). This assignment recognizes the value
of revising a completed draft without the stress of an open-ended
total revision. The workshop model emphasizes the ongoing conversation writers have with their own work, even after submission.
I prefer the workshop because it presupposes a draft in progress.
In the rare case that a writer turns in a hastily composed final
draft, a rushed full-draft rewrite would undermine the important
conversation that a writer needs to have (and should have had)
with the material. Requiring a discrete revision assignment of all
writers, regardless of their grade, signals that all work is ongoing
and can benefit from post-draft revision.

To emphasize revision as an ongoing conversation, I devote
three class meetings (or nearly two weeks of class time) to conversations that include conferences and an activity called "conversation
extension" (appendix 7). Having completed the rough draft, writers
identify a person in the field—sometimes a professional, sometimes a family member or friend with expertise in the area—with
whom they can share their claim. One of my students was writing
about ecofeminism and sent an email to Annette Kolodny, a well-
known scholar in that field. The student asked a specific question
regarding her own claim, and Kolodny took the time to respond.
The exchange invigorated and challenged the student, ultimately
giving her deeper insight into her own work. (Not all scholars
would be as willing or able to answer emails from students, but it
is always worth a try.) Another student spoke to the president of a
local Sierra Club chapter about local wastewater issues, while still

another spoke to the leader of a Mexican feminist organization. The exercise asks writers to move away from their immediate surroundings, and it encourages them to see the potential of their work beyond the confines of the classroom.

These conversations are not intended to be interviews, but rather serious dialogues and catalysts for examination and revision that take place prior to final draft submission. Whether these conversations offer surprising new views or confirm the writer's own claims, they connect writers to lived experience. One writer spoke to her pastor about her research into community gardens as a potential site of hospitality and worship. She discovered that he, too, was thinking about the potential for a community garden. She was able to share her research, and he was able to discuss the practical obstacles with her. Together they toured the church property to assess potential garden locations. The student's research will have an impact outside our classroom because of her conversation with this pastor. If the writers have practiced the art of listening and attention throughout the research process, their conversations are often fruitful and dynamic.

In our final days together as a class, the writers gather in a circle to discuss their conversation extension experiences. They summarize their topics, describe why they chose their conversation partner, and share how the conversation affected their thinking. The other writers ask questions, interjecting observations and connections of their own. That the conversation extensions come full circle to generate conversation in our classroom is one of my favorite outcomes. It is not unusual for writers to leave these discussions with new questions or new potential topics to research, nor is it unusual for writers to depart with a greater respect for and connection to one another.

Shared Hopes: Listening to One Another

Open-minded conversations leave the door open for difference and growth, the stuff of stronger, more vibrant communities. Even in a world where we can customize our newsfeeds and where algorithms influence the content we see, new ideas will surely reach us. When we prepare to meet new or opposing ideas with openness, we invite the kind of intellectual friction that sparks not just debate but imagination and progress. Writers who cultivate open-mindedness see potential in the dialectic space between ideas and people, and they are more willing to engage with that tension and emerge with new ideas. And yet, being open-minded does not mean that we cannot have, and keep, strong beliefs. Intellectual humility need not mean that we are spineless, or that we change beliefs with every strong intellectual wind that blows; it means that we listen deeply to other points of view, try to articulate opposition with compassion, and work to bring out the best insights in others as well as ourselves.

In addition to teaching Twentieth Century American Literature, I teach two team-style courses, including Composition. Though I love the autonomy of teaching alone, the collaboration involved in team teaching consistently impresses and invigorates me. We come together with the same goals, but we all have different experiences and perspectives about pedagogy, assignment design, scheduling— any number of details large or small. As I learned in a grocery store halfway across the world, though, my way is not the only or right way of doing things. It is just *a* way of doing things. Listening to my colleagues with an open mind improves me as a teacher, thinker, writer, and friend. My brilliant colleague Grete prepares her syllabi differently than I do, approaches the classroom differently, and often designs assignments differently. In fact, her version of an exercise was so helpful in reframing a concept for me that I requested her permission to share it, not only because it makes a strong point about being open-minded but also because it helps writers practice assessing open-mindedness. We both ask writers to write a short response describing a time when they changed their minds, and we ask them to discuss what contributed to that change. My assignment stopped there, but Grete suggested that it would be helpful to have them respond to an additional question: What is something you would not change your mind about, and what might it take to sway you? She observes that when writers respond that nothing could change their minds, returning to the first response (about a time they *did* change their minds) leads to interesting and compelling discussion. This activity prompts writers to go beyond recounting an instance of open-mindedness to consider the limits of that openness as well.

In my other team-taught course, Humanities, we curate the syllabus and assignments together, and though we teach individual sections, we also write corporate exams. Together, we navigate perspectives from our different fields and personal experience in our classrooms. Though the work is not easy and is sometimes frustrating, it is some of the most rewarding work that I do. I am a decidedly better teacher because of this collegial conversation. On the page and in conversation, intellectually humble thinkers "find the right balance between dogmatically rejecting the dissenting viewpoints of others and yielding too quickly in the face of intellectual conflict."[19] Writers find that balance through a combination of research and time. Being an open-minded writer means reading widely and carefully, seeking out different voices and experiences that can cross-pollinate one another. It means opening ourselves not just to revision of drafts, but to revising our ideas as well.

---

19. Krumrei-Mancuso and Rouse, "Comprehensive Intellectual Humility Scale," 209.

seven

Be Generous

When my students identified generosity as a key component of good conversation, they tapped into a complicated human quality, one that necessarily implies relationship and concern for others. Scholars have long studied the puzzling science of generosity, which by prioritizing the welfare of a group contradicts the common assumption that human nature involves selfishness and competition. Whatever we might think about human nature, scholars who study generosity find it is an integral part of human behavior.[1] The University of Notre Dame sponsors a "Science of Generosity" initiative that explores generosity as an "essential human virtue." The Notre Dame initiative traces the cultural roots of generosity to a "nobility of spirit," and ultimately defines generosity as "giving good things freely and abundantly."[2] While that definition

1. Greater Good Science Center, "Science of Generosity," 2018, white paper prepared for the John Templeton Foundation, University of California, Berkeley, pp. 9–15, https://www.templeton.org/wp-content/uploads/2018/01/Generosity_White _Paper-FinalJTF.pdf.
2. "What Is Generosity?," Science of Generosity, University of Notre Dame, accessed February 2022, https://generosityresearch.nd.edu/more-about-the -initiative/what-is-generosity.

might resonate with charitable giving or "moral orientation to life,"[3] it may not immediately and clearly connect with academic or scholarly work. Universities function as important contributors to overall public knowledge, scholarship, and scientific discovery, but they have not always cultivated a generous spirit or relationship with those outside academia. Tuition costs have skyrocketed and admissions criteria can be onerous and prohibitive. Research resources are often unavailable to the public, and academic conferences cater to academic scholars, often featuring only panelists from well-known institutions. Even the playful yet pejorative nickname "the ivory tower" conveys a perception of higher education as disconnected and exclusive. Yet, as scientists have discovered, generosity is just as much a part of who we are as is curiosity. Institutionally, universities and colleges can do more to cultivate a spirit of academic generosity, but that good work begins in daily conversational practice, something of particular interest in the writing classroom and applicable in all areas of study.

I would venture that we all know someone who is a generous thinker and conversationalist. Generous conversationalists ask interesting, open-ended questions and make room for others to speak. Amy, the young woman mentioned in chapter 1, embodies all these qualities with her curiosity and attention. She engages in meaningful conversations in and out of the classroom, always ready to ask a thoughtful question and listen carefully to the response. One of my colleagues in political science, also named Amy, often brings the gift of generous thinking to the conversation. She works to set aside her own intellectual ego and consider multiple points of view, an especially important model for her students. Indeed, though it may not be the academic stereotype, many of my colleagues demonstrate the same kind of openness and humility.

Being conversationally generous means cultivating all those traits previously discussed—from curiosity to open-mindedness. The composition classroom can model this relationship and

3. "What Is Generosity?"

community-building work by intentionally seeking and sharing knowledge beyond the classroom. A generosity-centered composition conversation promotes access to knowledge and discussion through further conversation, citation, and presentation. The conversation extension exercise (appendix 7) is one practical way to move the conversation beyond the classroom. Doing so challenges the "construction of certain forms of knowledge as always and only available to the elite."[4] The conversation extension is also important because it forces writers to re-evaluate their conversational approach. Speaking to someone with lived experience may require a different register or tone than speaking to a friend or a professor. The formal academic style is far less important in those conversations than is a strong command of the research or the ability to articulate concisely a position on the topic.

Benevolent Bibliography: The Generosity of Citation

Another form of generosity comes from clear citation. Citation has a long history of attributing credit to the original thinker and of establishing the research credentials of the writer. Many citation guides indicate that careful citation lends credibility, but it also lends transparency to the writer's own thought process. Perhaps the most important element of citation, however, is the democratization of the research process. Clear internal citation followed by a well-ordered bibliography offers a reader access to the same material, inviting that reader into the conversation. Princeton history professor Anthony Grafton, the author of several works about footnotes, highlights the generosity involved in citation: "Devised to give texts authority, footnotes in fact undermine. They democratize scholarly writing: they bring many voices, including those of the sources, together on a single page. . . . The reader hears, and even takes part in, a conversation, with the author and the

4. hooks, *Teaching Community*, 41.

author's witnesses alike."[5] Approaching citation as another form of conversational hospitality refocuses its purpose away from preventing plagiarism or asserting authority and toward an invitation to discussion.

The democratization of scholarly writing is my favorite outcome of citation, the one I stress to students. When we join scholarly conversations in progress and invite others along with us, we acknowledge that understanding evolves and grows with each new voice and that we have not proclaimed the final word on a topic. The generosity and transparency involved in citation signals our commitment to developing ideas in conversation. Citation allows us to give credit to those whose thinking and research has framed our own, and citation allows us to detail our own research journeys—what we have and have not considered. Plagiarism, which is often explained as intellectual theft, also robs us of the opportunity for more comprehensive conversation because it eliminates this dynamic interaction. Like any generous conversation, citation requires work and vulnerability.

Giving Good Things Freely: Conference Presentations

Careful citation invites readers to be part of the conversation, but that participation is more theoretical than concrete. To demonstrably realize these conversations, writers need opportunities to present and disseminate their work. For many scholars, academic conferences provide those opportunities. At their best, conferences encourage a spirit of collaboration. Writer and climate advocate Kim Stanley Robinson has great faith in academic conferences to move us toward substantive and positive change, and nearly all his science fiction books feature some sort of scholarly conference where people come together to cultivate new ideas. Many years ago, at the beginning of my teaching career, I emerged from a

5. Grafton, "Death of the Footnote," 77.

scholarly conference abuzz with the creative energy of collaboration. As I drove the many miles back to my home, I realized that students rarely have that experience: they seldom have opportunities to present their own ideas and also bear witness to the ideas of their peers. Since that time, the composition faculty at my college have hosted an annual writing conference in lieu of a final exam. The registrar graciously granted us a corporate exam time to make it possible for all composition students to attend. In our two-hour exam time, we host a conference focused on the corporate CFP (appendix 1) assigned to students at the beginning of the semester. We are able to feature four or five panels, each with three presenters and a faculty moderator. The CFP thematically orients writers of many different interests and scholarly fields, allowing panels to emerge quite organically and to coalesce around subtopics such as education, ministry, or engineering. Participants sign up for the panel that most interests them (appendix 8). Instructors name and moderate each panel, modeling generous discussion practices throughout. Attendees fill out a simple response sheet (appendix 9) as they listen, using these notes to craft questions that drive the post-presentation discussion. Because student engagement is high, the post-presentation conference discussion rivals and sometimes even surpasses that of the professional conferences I have attended.

One reason the discussion soars is that the writers have invested in one another as part of a composition community. Writers often note in their conference evaluations that having experienced the rigor of the work together deepens their respect for the exceptional projects presented. Similarly, writers often find connections to their own work that inspire them to ask new and different questions or make new connections. Unlike some professional academic conferences, the panels focus always on celebration rather than competition, though that does not mean that healthy critique is not allowed. To achieve this kind of dynamic dialogue, instructors prepare all writers to present and attend. Just as a good theater production requires a skilled stage crew and an engaged audience in addition to great performances, a successful scholarly conference requires more than strong scholarship.

The Stage Crew (Panel Moderators)

We invite instructors to moderate panels in which they have a strong interest or on which they have one or more presenting students. Some years, I moderate panels that deeply interest me, such as foodways panels or environmental justice panels, while other years, I moderate panels with which I have little experience, but which feature students whose work I know intimately. Either way, I am poised to guide and direct the conversation throughout the panel. The moderators are also responsible for meeting with their panelists, helping them prepare their presentations, and making sure all the presentation technology works without a glitch. Moderators play an important support role in the overall success of each panel discussion.

The Engaged Audience (Panel Attendees)

As any actor can attest, performing for a disengaged or hostile audience can mitigate months of preparation and ruin a show. Before the conference, all writers—regardless of their role as attendee or presenter—practice asking good questions. One helpful activity to promote engagement encourages all writers to spend ten to fifteen minutes responding to the following prompts:

- What one question would I like to be asked about my project and why?
- What one question would I hate to be asked about my project and why?

In discussion, we find that writers often want to be asked about research they found interesting but did not fit into the confines of their project, or what they would research as a next step. In contrast, writers do not want to be asked questions on adjacent topics they have not studied at all. Inviting all writers, regardless of whether they are presenting, to reflect in this way generates empathy and, ultimately, more compelling discussion during the conference. We also identify types of questions that are sometimes posed in these situations, and we work to avoid or embrace them as needed.

- **The Show-Off Question,** usually framed as a "humblebrag," shows how much the questioner knows about the topic. This type of question rarely leads to meaningful discussion because it is self-focused.
- **The Clarifying Question** invites the presenter to clear up a misunderstanding or confusion. These kinds of questions can be helpful, but they can also be accusatory or mean-spirited. Working to frame all questions with compassion can elevate this question to an opportunity for dialogue.
- **The Too-Personal Question** usually focuses on a writer's personal history or motivations for choosing the topic. While the answer can provide interesting background, it is often a question better asked one-on-one because the personal nature of the response can shut down further dialogue.
- **The Incomprehensible Question:** In the NBC comedy *The Office*, manager Michael Scott invents something called the "improversation," in which he starts a sentence and simply hopes it will find its way on its own.[6] Even at scholarly conferences, I have heard participants frame truly incomprehensible questions full of big words, complicated clauses, and probably semicolons as they listen to

6. *The Office*, season 5, episode 12, "The Duel," directed by Dean Holland, written by Jennifer Celotta, aired January 15, 2009, on NBC.

themselves talk and hope to find their question along the way. I have watched gracious and generous presenters consider thoughtfully and respond, "What I think I hear you saying is . . ." and then reframe a more answerable question. Taking notes and crafting written questions throughout the panel helps attendees achieve conversation rather than "improversation."

• **The Generous Question:** Like the great conversationalists we know, this question makes room for more discussion. It is usually open-ended and born of careful attention. In the best scenario, it inspires connections to other projects or new questions.

The Great Performance (Panel Presentations)

To facilitate strong discussion and engagement, presenters need guidance. In the days before the conference, a presenter works with the moderator to prepare an engaging presentation. Strong presentations require distillation, practice, question anticipation, and poise. When I first began attending conferences, and even when we first began hosting the writing conference, presenters would stand at the front of the room and read their papers aloud. After careful drafting and revision, reading aloud seems a fitting tribute to the work given to such craftsmanship. And yet, reading a long argument aloud may not be the best way to connect with or engage listeners. Moderators work with presenters to help them distill their presentations where necessary by thinking about the presentation in sections and building slide presentations to accompany their work. Writers learn to create captivating visual presentations that feature some of their main arguments, and they choose portions of their project to read as they present their work. Each slide should be simple, featuring only a major point or a single quotation, illustration, or graph.

Presenters also work with moderators to practice their presentations in advance. Each panelist has twenty minutes for presentation and questions, and presenters need to work to ensure that they do not go over (or significantly under) the time allotted. Most double-spaced, typed pages take approximately two minutes to read aloud at an average pace. Writers who have written fifteen to twenty pages need to condense some of their work, which means some of their written work might be abridged, making practice sessions even more important. Practicing can also alert writers to passages that might read well silently but not aloud, giving them the opportunity to revise for flow and tone. Most importantly, practicing breeds the kind of confidence most likely to engage listeners well.

After practicing the actual presentation, presenters can prepare by anticipating possible audience questions. Prior to the presentation, moderators meet with writers to develop a list of ten questions they might be asked. This process encourages writers to think about blind spots in their argument, as well as tangential or interesting topics likely to generate curiosity. As writers develop and anticipate questions, moderators encourage them to become familiar with their own bibliography, noting which texts might be most helpful to those with further interest or questions. Of course, no writer will be able to answer or even anticipate all the possible questions that a presentation might generate, which is why we also encourage writers to admit when they do not know an answer. Language such as "That is an interesting question, but it wasn't part of my study" or "I would have to do more research to answer that question well" can help writers acknowledge the limits of their project without feeling inadequate.

Most writers have experience giving presentations or speeches of some kind, but it never hurts to reiterate how a writer's poise can impact a presentation. Some writers excel at public speaking, but some pale at the thought of it, even (or especially) when addressing their peers. Technology allows us to live stream the conference to family and friends across the country, which can make the experience even more nerve-racking. We encourage panelists to dress professionally but comfortably, a sort of "look-good,

feel-good" approach to presentation. Professional dress signals a
writer's respect for the topic and the event, expressing the ethos
they learned about at the beginning of their writing journey. With
practice, the other elements of good speaking fall into place: eye
contact, pacing, inflection. Because the classroom has been a site
of generous interaction, the panels themselves provide a similar
atmosphere, helping presenters to relax and settle into the celebration of good work done well.

Throughout the conference, writers extend generosity to one another through attention, preparation, engagement, and response.
These steps provide generous entry and access to the assembled
students, professors, family, and friends. When we first launched
the composition conference years ago, we considered a prize for
the best paper, thinking perhaps that we had to entice students
to write well. I am so glad we instead trusted students to enter
into meaningful dialogue and discover the value of research and
writing for themselves. One of the final questions on the conference response sheet asks, "What was the most valuable part of
the conference experience?" Each year, attendees consistently
respond that they appreciate the opportunity to hear new ideas
and make connections to their own work. In short, they appreciate
the chance to dialogue with one another, a reward no monetary
prize could match.

Sharing work at conferences or in publication can be a form
of generosity, but unless we share our work as part of ongoing
dialogue, it is a limited one. Too often, sharing our work becomes
more about a personality parade, bound up in ego and self-esteem.
Writing emerges from our personal experience of the world, and
it can feel like the most private enterprise, but at its best, writing is the work of and in community. Anne Lamott observes that
if we are not "enough" before publication or presentation, those
recognitions will not make us "enough."[7] Generosity reminds us
to write in search of truth, not accolades. One of the reasons I am

7. Lamott, *Bird by Bird*, 220.

so proud of our writing conference is precisely because it is not a competition. When we gather at the conference, we celebrate the culmination of everyone's hard work, and everyone has a stake in the conversation.

Generous Curiosity: Ongoing Research

The conversations stimulated by research, the extension project, and the conference catapult writers toward new ideas. Sometimes, after weeks of research, writers can finally articulate a stronger entry into their original topic, and sometimes their work dialoguing with evidence and with other writers helps generate a new idea. The final assignment of my writing course asks writers to spend some time thinking about these potential new directions. In the ongoing research proposal assignment (appendix 10), writers craft a new research question and complete the initial elements of a research proposal. In addition, they identify a potential project mentor on campus, someone whose expertise in the area could help guide and frame their work if they choose to move forward with the project. They spend time considering materials needed, a potential budget for their research, and even a possible conference for presentation. Writers have no obligation to complete the research they propose, but many do decide to pursue these projects, and some have gone on to present at national undergraduate conferences to great success. Whether or not these writers pursue their hypothetical projects, they leave the course thinking about questions instead of answers. The ongoing research proposal suggests, I hope, that inquiry motivates education, and that curiosity carries us deeper toward truth and into the world.

Sometimes writing toward truth may mean conflict with ourselves and with others. Rachel Held Evans provoked controversy with her challenges to the evangelical Christian tradition. Reflecting on her work, Jason Byassee notes that she listened to theologians on the margins, she was a "bridge builder" who sparked and tended conversation, and she was not afraid to admit when she was wrong or when she found something valuable in an alternative position.[8] Evans tacked motivational reminders to the walls of her writing space, including "one true sentence" and "tell the truth." The power of those directives sent her to the Scriptures, to the library, and to her community for what would become a lifelong pursuit—not of answers, but of increasingly complex questions. Every writer and thinker I have cited throughout this book shares a similar commitment to asking and listening. All writers can benefit from these models of generous curiosity.

No True Words Alone: Writing in Community

Generosity has a long history as a cultural and moral virtue, and the characteristics associated with generosity, such as selflessness, mutuality, and hospitality, inform good conversation and good writing. Cultivating a spirit of generosity often means recognizing the need for change, whether within ourselves or in the world. Paolo Freire, in his *Pedagogy of the Oppressed*, writes that "to speak a true word is to transform the world."[9] Yet Freire also stresses the importance of reflection and listening for true transformative discourse. Writers must acknowledge the "right of everyone" to speak a true word, and that "no one can say a true word alone."[10] The danger in what might feel like a righteous cause—to transform the world—can sometimes become what Freire identifies as a "prescriptive act" where we presume to speak for others.[11] The writing classroom provides a unique opportunity to practice speaking and listening in community. As we gather research and disparate points of view, we turn toward synthesis rather than

8. Jason Byassee, "Rachel Held Evans: Public Theologian," *Christian Century*, August 27, 2019, https://www.christiancentury.org/article/critical-essay/rachel-held-evans-public-theologian.

9. Freire, *Pedagogy of the Oppressed*, 87.

10. Freire, *Pedagogy of the Oppressed*, 88.

11. Freire, *Pedagogy of the Oppressed*, 88.

prescription, recognizing again and again that we do not yet know what we do not know.

Generosity is at the heart of every meaningful and transformative conversation. Generosity helps us listen instead of simply waiting to talk. When we need to say or understand hard things about one another, ourselves, or the world, generosity allows us to engage new ideas without suspicion or hostility. And though being generous is part of who we are, it is not always our first instinct. Cultivating virtues such as curiosity, attentiveness, and empathy brings us deeper into relationship, a crucial step in navigating thorny issues. In the case of climate change, for example, Katharine Hayhoe knows that having hard conversations can be divisive. Instead of pummeling her audiences with facts and figures, she models generosity in speaking and writing. She works to develop relationships first, listening to find common ground. Despite the urgency and politicization of the climate change issue, her book is not titled *Saving the Earth* but rather *Saving Us*. Part of that redemption includes humble discourse in which cultivating common ground yields more fruitful discussions. These days, it may feel as if common ground is in short supply, but that scarcity is a myth. Generosity can reveal how much we really do share, even and especially when we disagree. Academic writing helps us practice and apply the types of conversational skills that matter in our everyday lives as well as our classrooms. Too often, general education requirements such as composition seem divorced from the "real world." But as bell hooks writes, "Schooling [is] always part of our real-world experience, our real life."[12] The hard work of writing well, with an aim to transform ourselves and others, matters more than ever—not in some far-flung academic future, but right now.

Writing with a conversational framework helps us see ourselves, as Ellen Ott Marshall writes, "within a web of relationships" that require accountability and dialogue.[13] When everyone has the

---

12. hooks, *Teaching Community*, 41.
13. Marshall, *Introduction to Christian Ethics*, 150.

right and the opportunity to speak a true word, we might feel uncomfortable as we listen to experiences different from our own, but if we are listening and speaking in community, this discomfort can develop stronger individual relationships as well as stronger, healthier community relationships. Approaching writing as an opportunity for self-reflection and growth, as a place to listen and speak true words in community, will first and foremost transform us, the necessary first step to transforming the world.

Conclusion

Be in Conversation

Framing writing as a conversation emphasizes intention and care, not only with words and language, but with the people behind the research, our dialogue partners, and ourselves. We have a responsibility to engage earnestly and in good faith with those who disagree with us as well as those who agree. As I was completing work on this book, the Republican National Convention withdrew from the Commission on National Debates, but as David Smith of *The Guardian* observes, the "value of debates has been questioned in this highly partisan, fragmented media age."[1] In a time when those who seek leadership and elected leaders from all parties are refusing to engage in civil debate (with or without the commission), we have even more reason and urgency to model and hone these skills in our own lives. Most political debates abandon the potential of a give-and-take conversation, and though candidates have long lists of talking points, they often do very little listening to one another or to their constituents. These types of debates often serve to entrench positions rather than move toward more comprehensive

1. David Smith, "What Does Republicans' Break from the Presidential Debate Commission Mean?," *The Guardian*, April 16, 2022, https://www.theguardian.com /us-news/2022/apr/16/republican-party-presidential-debate-commission-withdraw.

understandings or even compromises. Of course, candidates need to distinguish themselves from the field of contenders, but practicing empathy and the ability to see the complexity of another position would signal the humility needed to lead a diverse nation.

In a much more intimate application, framing writing as a conversation in the classroom encourages writers to listen before they speak. The work of listening and writing, though it usually involves sitting at a desk, feels strangely physical. Writers wrestle complex ideas to the page, grapple with data, and craft new perspectives. It is no wonder that a day of writing can leave writers energized but physically exhausted. Only after listening attentively can we acknowledge the nuance required for this work. We also tend to think of writing as solitary work—sitting at that same desk waiting for genius to strike. A conversational approach to writing helps reframe writing as a communal endeavor. Writing an academic paper—writing anything, really—means seeking out and listening to experienced voices around us before we enter the conversation. A conversational framework puts a human face on the other side of the page, raising the relational stakes of our endeavors. The writers who attend the composition conference each year question one another respectfully and out of genuine curiosity precisely because they have humanized the writing process. Not only have all the participants experienced the hard work of writing, but they have also been in conversation with one another throughout the semester. Developing a cogent, objective position requires far more humility than contention, something we do more instinctively in conversation than anywhere else. As Krista Tippett writes, "Once I have a sense of your experience, you and I are in relationship, acknowledging the complexity in each other's position, listening less guardedly."[2] She does not mean that we listen less attentively, but instead with a looser grip on our own territory. Good conversation brings us into relationship, and once we are in relationship it is harder to dismiss one another's experience. Thinking about

2. Tippett, *Becoming Wise*, 22.

writing in this way can extend the kind of relationship we have with our studies and with our communities.

Writing is hard work. A student recently sat in my office and said, "I hate writing. I just wish there was a clear process, a formula I could follow." Of course, writing *does* have a process, but it isn't fixed. Like any conversation, the process, the approach, the preparation all depend on the situation and the topic. My student knows instinctively how to approach a conversation about last night's Vols win with his buddies, just as he knows that a conversation with his family about finances requires a different tone and data. When I likened writing to these kinds of conversations, he groaned, "But that is so hard." Listening, responding, researching well—these are all hard work, but they facilitate transformative conversations worth pursuing. As one of the great delights of my teaching, I am watching as this student commits to that work, despite its difficulty.

This book is certainly not a final word on how to enter the writing conversation; I may make important discoveries and revisions before it even comes to publication. This book is, however, an appeal to enter and remain in conversation, to take our writing opportunities seriously as sites of genuine conversation, and to keep asking questions even if the answers are hard or elusive. Every year, I listen to and learn from my colleagues and students, making adjustments where needed. The syllabus may change every year, but the principles of conversation hold, and I am grateful to the many young women and men in my classes who see the value in listening, attention, and generosity. It is a privilege to be in conversation with them. Writing is indeed hard work, but it is, and can be, meaningful work at any stage—whether it is my daughter's fifth grade research, a doctoral dissertation, or a college writing assignment. When we enter the writing process willing to be surprised, we might just surprise ourselves as we emerge with a more nuanced understanding of ourselves.

APPENDIX 1

Sample Call for Papers

Sustainability: Building Webs of Interdependence

The complexity of global concerns continues to increase—whether in the form of truly global crises such as new diseases in need of cures or vaccines and philosophical dilemmas about our response to technology, or more local issues such as the impact of climate change on the Tennessee Valley or the ability to retain qualified teachers in a local county. Norman Wirzba, in his book *Paradise of God*, discusses the "webs of interdependence" that connect all things and people.[1] For Wirzba, it isn't enough to be good stewards, but we must also be innovative and creative to allow others to flourish in life-giving and life-sustaining contexts. This kind of sustainability is both forward- and backward-looking, and it addresses far more than simply environmental concerns.

Students should explore sustainability through their specific fields of study or interests. For example, students might consider the sustainability of intense, perhaps faddish workout or food regimens

---

1. Norman Wirzba, *The Paradise of God: Renewing Religion in an Ecological Age* (Oxford: Oxford University Press, 2007), 77.

for a healthy lifestyle and planet. Similarly, they might question whether advertised sustainability in product sales is another extension of consumerism or to what extent the pace of modern life is sustainable. This inquiry need not assume that sustainability is inherently "good" or "bad." In fact, the investigation need not arrive at an overtly moralistic declaration on the topic, and students might instead elect to remain impartial. In either case, the best essays will take a nuanced approach in their treatment of this complex subject.

Sample Research Problems and Questions[2]

1. As church leaders in various denominations and movements seek to apply the principles of church growth to their congregations, churches often tend to embrace models of community that derive from the world of business and other large organizations. This can lead to churches that are heavy in the implementation of new programs, and dependent on those at the top—those designated as having certain levels of expertise—to "run the church." Authors such as Chris Smith and John Pattison (*Slow Church*) and Tim Suttle (*Shrink: Faithful Ministry in a Church-Growth Culture*) conclude that, while the result of these church-growth techniques might be a smoothly functioning organization, much is lost when church members are not encouraged to take ownership in the church's ministries, instead becoming consumers of the programs that various congregations offer. In addition, these approaches often lead congregations to view one another as competitors within the marketplace of potential members, rather than coworkers in God's kingdom. When interdependence among church members and among different congregations is abandoned for principles of competition and a reliance on experts, is church

2. Questions 1 through 3 were contributed by Dr. Todd Edmondson, Dr. Michael Blouin, and Dr. Daniel Silliman, respectively.

growth sustainable? How does the church's mission suffer when such models become the norm?

2. Hollywood films frequently critique environmental destruction. Recent popular examples include *Avatar* (2009), *Snowpiercer* (2013), and *Maleficent* (2014). Yet, despite their broad appeal, a call to arms by these films has not translated into effective social action. Specifically, this paper will consider the disaster film *The Day after Tomorrow* (2004). How does the film represent environmental sustainability? Does it model an alternative framework? And in what ways might one account for an impasse between the film's message and real-world change?

3. In research conducted over the past few years, Timothy McGuine, a senior scientist and research coordinator at the University of Wisconsin Health Sports Medicine Center, found that children who specialize early in sports (such as elite baseball travel teams or gymnastics) were 50 percent more likely to be injured.[3] Some of these injuries require surgery and may lead to lifelong problems such as the ulnar ligament damage many baseball pitchers experience in their shoulders. The American Orthopedic Society even weighed in to say that the risk outweighed the benefit for early specialization. Yet according to research published in the National Strength and Conditioning Association, single-sport athletes are increasing every year. If there is indeed no benefit to early specialization, how can parents and coaches reframe the youth sports experience? And if athletes continue to specialize despite the risks, in what ways can parents, coaches, and young athletes work together to ensure that youth sport participation is sustainable and healthy into adulthood?

---

3. Timothy A. McGuine, Eric G. Post, Scott J. Hetzel, M. Alison Brooks, Stephanie Trigsted, and David R. Bell, "A Prospective Study on the Effect of Sport Specialization on Lower Extremity Injury Rates in High School Athletes," *American Journal of Sports Medicine* 45, no. 12 (July 23, 2017): 2706–12, https://doi.org/10.1177/0363546517710213.

APPENDIX 2

Research Proposal Template

Section 1: Topic, Motivation, and Value of the Study

- *Introduce your research topic and explain why you have chosen it*—What is the problem? What is at stake? What motivates you to write about this topic? How does this topic connect to the larger call for papers?
- *Describe the academic value of your research project*—for others, as well as yourself. Why is this research project of interest and worth doing? What do you hope to gain from it? How do you think you or others may be able to use or benefit from your research findings? To which specific community could it be helpful?

Section 2: Research Topic Problem and Question (see samples in the CFP)

- *Establish problem/context and draft the research question*—The answer to these questions will eventually become your thesis. The research problem and questions will also help you determine which sources fit your topic. A research question should *not* be answered with a finite or quantifiable response (e.g., yes, no, 42). That is, your question should be complex and allow for exploration and sometimes multiple answers.

- *Related questions*—What other questions connect to your leading research question?

  These questions might be more specific or detailed.

Section 3: Entering the Conversation

To enter the conversation, you need a well-defined point of departure for your research project and a clear sense of direction provided by substantial, promising, exploratory research and serious, preliminary thinking and reading.

- *Understanding the conversation:* To contribute to a dialogue, you must know what others are saying. Provide here a list of experts or strong voices in the field and a brief summary of their arguments.
- *Anticipate counterarguments:* What might be the counterarguments to your approach? Provide a thoughtful and brief discussion of those counterarguments here. You will expand on this section later in the research process.

Section 4: Research Plan

This section should indicate clear thinking and progress with respect to your research.

- *List the search terms* you are using.
- *List the places you will conduct most of your research,* such as specific databases and journals of interest, stacks, archives, surveys—discuss all that apply.

- *Decide which documentation style you will use* and provide justification for that decision.

Section 5: Preliminary Research

- *Provide a bibliographic citation and annotation for two sources from your preliminary library research* and list any others that look like they might help. Your annotation should offer a summary of the ideas and comment on how the source might be useful to your project. These two sources will be the first entries in your annotated bibliography.

APPENDIX 3

Annotated Bibliography Guide

- Format heading according to assignment style guide (MLA, APA, CMS, or other)
- Read and assess ten sources
  - ▸ Include at least two peer-reviewed journal articles
  - ▸ Include at least one book, but no sacred texts or textbooks
  - ▸ Note: sources may exceed ten for the project, but include only ten on the assignment
- Use correct bibliographic citations in alphabetical order with hanging indentation
- Use single-spaced annotations, with spaces between each individual entry
- Annotation tips:
  - ▸ Provide a brief summary of major arguments and approach
  - ▸ Address any concerns about the timeliness or bias of the article (optional/not always necessary)

- ▸ Give rationale for use in your work or connection to certain arguments you want to make
- ▸ Make connections to other sources in the bibliography
- ▸ Avoid quotations—the annotation is for making connections, not pointed arguments of your own
- ▸ Annotations should run from approximately 100 to 200 words each
- Include running page/header

APPENDIX 4

Peer Review Interview and Peer Review Guide

Peer Interview

This interview should be conducted with your partner prior to the peer review.

1. What is your connection to this topic? Why did it interest you?
2. What do you want to argue in this essay, and how do you think that argument contributes to the conversation around this topic?
3. What do you think is your strongest argument or section? What evidence contributes most to the strength?
4. What dialogue, either with the evidence or with another scholar, expanded your thinking in this essay?
5. Where would you like me to focus my critique as I read your essay?

Directions

1. Read and comment on the draft according to the guide below.
2. Offer at least **one positive comment** and **three constructive comments** in the margins or at the end of the piece. Also include **one question** you have for the writer. The question can be about something you do not understand, something you would like to know more about, or a connection you would like the writer to consider.
3. Rate the overall strength of the paper on a scale of 1–100 using the scoring system below.

Peer Review Guidelines

- Underline the thesis sentence of this essay. Evaluate the claim: Is it arguable? Does it make a unique claim?
- Circle ideas, claims, and transitions that work well.
- Indicate passages that are unclear in content (that is, they need to be "unpacked," developed, or analyzed more completely).
- Highlight passages that are stylistically unclear (preposition trains, unwieldy syntax, etc.).
- Respond to the use of evidence in the paper: More? Less? Better integrations?
- After reading the paper, do you agree or disagree with the writer's claim? Why or why not?

1. Introduction	1–10	___
2. Thesis	1–10	___
3. Evidence, dialogue with sources	1–10	___
4. Style (sentence work/diction)	1–10	___
5. Transitions	1–10	___

6. Topic claims	1–10	___
7. End of paragraph synthesis	1–10	___
8. Connects to CFP	1–10	___
9. Original, clear argument	1–10	___
10. Conclusion	1–10	___
	Total	___

Introduction and conclusion comparison: Read the introduction followed immediately by the conclusion. Mark your responses on the draft.

1. Write down the major claims of the introduction. Do you find these claims fulfilled in the conclusion?
2. Which introduction claims resonate most powerfully in the conclusion?
3. Are any introduction claims lost in the conclusion?
4. Read the conclusion carefully and read the intro thesis carefully—sometimes the conclusion offers a better thesis than the intro. If this is the case, put stars around the "thesis-type" sentence in the conclusion.
5. In terms of balance (development, reader engagement, physical space on the page), how does the conclusion compare to the introduction?
6. In your conference with the writer, be prepared to describe what you found most effective and what you found most ineffective in this draft (no need to give advice, just respond as a reader).

APPENDIX 5

Research Essay Guided Revision

Task 1

1. Identify the section you would like me to see in class for our mini-conference.
2. Note which instructor or peer comments you addressed in revision.

Task 2

1. Review any relevant style manual on the process of integrating quotations.
2. Evaluate each of the quotations you used in your draft and ensure that each one is integrated smoothly, introduced adequately, and cited accurately.
3. Review all your citations, internal and on the Works Cited page.
4. Check each internal citation to see if the source has page numbers and cite where appropriate.

5. Make sure each internal citation has corresponding Works Cited representation.

Task 3

1. Read your introduction and your conclusion in succession.
2. Make sure your conclusion echoes the trajectory of the intro and extends your ideas beyond those initial claims.
3. The conclusion should take up questions such as:
   a. What is at stake?
   b. What should be considered further?
   c. What is to be expected (given these conditions, new understanding, etc.)?

Task 4

1. Choose one paragraph to read *lectio* style.
2. Make notes about coherence, word choice, cohesion. Change or admire as needed!

Task 5

1. Evaluate your title. Does it offer a CFP-related scope? Do you need help with this before you leave?
2. Identify a section that has cohesion issues and read aloud. You may leave (briefly—5 minutes or so) with your draft for the stairwell or the porch to accomplish this task. Take a pen and a paper draft.

Task 6

1. Identify 2 sections you will polish before the final draft and schedule a time to work on them.
2. Read the draft for punctuation, spelling, formatting, and grammar errors.

APPENDIX 6

Revision Workshop Template

Directions: Complete the following revisions based on original essay score. Attach any new documents to this sheet. Every writer must complete the workshop for a homework grade in addition to the possible points recovered on the essay.

Essay score 90–100: Complete section A (possible +1 on essay)

Essay score 78–89: Complete sections A and B (possible +2 on essay)

Essay score 77 or below: Complete sections A, B, and C (possible +4 on essay)

Section A: More Elegance

Rationale: Essays that earn 90 or more points usually have clear arguments and strong analysis, but they can often benefit from more nuanced or precise syntax.

Goal: Choose *two* sentences in the draft that could benefit from the grace and clarity advocated by Joseph Williams. Copy the old sentences below, diagnose them, revise, and then evaluate your changes.

1. Sentence:
2. Diagnosis:
3. Revision:

1. Sentence:
2. Diagnosis:
3. Revision:

Evaluate your revised presentation.

Section B: Stronger Arguments, Clearer Ideas

Rationale: Essays that score between 78–89 often have a sound premise, but sometimes rely too heavily on summary or confuse good ideas with muddled syntax.

Goal: Choose *one* point where the idea is present but vague or generalized. Work to improve the depth of analysis. Focus can be on syntax as well as content.

Copy the old section below (copy/paste into new Word document is fine). **Use track changes** to demonstrate the progress of your revisions. **Evaluate** the revised version.

Section C: Paragraph Architecture and Development

Rationale: Essays that score below 77 points often need work on essay foundations—analytical ideas, sentence cohesion, paragraph coherence, and overall organization or direction.

Goal: Choose just one paragraph. Diagnose the problem of the paragraph. Identify the main idea of the paragraph. Draft a clear topic claim. Revise the paragraph, paying close attention to the sentence transitions, evidence, and closing sentence. **Evaluate** your changes.

1. Identify paragraph and copy into a new document.
2. Diagnose paragraph problem(s).
3. Identify main idea.
4. Revise topic claim that reflects the main idea.
5. Use track changes to demonstrate the progress of your revisions.
6. Evaluate the new paragraph in comparison to the old.

APPENDIX 7

Conversation Extension Plan

Meaningful research extends beyond the walls of your instructor's office and classroom assignments. The conversation extension asks you to participate in the academic conversation rather than simply repeating it—I want your research to matter, not just to me or you, but to the community and to others as well.

Conversation extension plans should begin as soon as you have a research proposal. The conversation extension process often generates new ideas and directions that can be incorporated into your final draft. Extending the conversation involves identifying someone (preferably off-campus, so that you might widen the scope of your conversation) with scholarly or lived experience who will talk to you about your project. Presentation of the process will occur in the last weeks of class, so keep good notes and records of your interactions.

- Identify your topic and your plan for extending the conversation. Offer a brief defense for this plan. Then discuss or list several things you hope to gain from your extension.

You might also consider questions you have or would like to discuss about your project with others who feel passionately about it.

- Your typed plan should include:
  - ▸ The person with whom you intend to extend the conversation
  - ▸ The person's/group's qualifications for extending that conversation
  - ▸ Timeline for completing the conversation extension
  - ▸ Method of interaction
- Presentation of the *completed* conversation extension will take place after the final draft is completed (as indicated on your syllabus). At that time, you will present (informally) the following:
  - ▸ A one-sentence summary of your topic/research
  - ▸ What you did to extend the conversation
  - ▸ What you learned
  - ▸ How "being part of the conversation" influenced your perception of the topic
- Participation in the conversation extension presentations will include asking questions of and making connections with your peers.

APPENDIX 8

Sample Conference Panel

Conference on Transformative Imagination

Panel 1: Music, Money, and Mental Health: Reimagining the Role of the Twenty-First-Century Church

Dr. Kayla Walker Edin, moderator

Elise Greene, "Mental Illness and Ministers: Imagining a Community of Vulnerability"

Mareena Rodriguez, "It's Nothing Personal: Reimagining the Business Model of the American Church"

Joseph Dykes, "Perspective and Poetry: Reimagining Twenty-First-Century American Hymnody"

Panel 2: The Imagination Age: Technology, Research, and a Healthy Community

Dr. Heather Hoover, moderator

Diego Carrasco, "Artificial Intelligence: An Innovative Technology for a Vital Industry"

Drake Shull, "What Doesn't Kill You Makes You Stronger: Using Disease to Treat Patients"

Doc Maines, "Viable Solutions to Climate Change"

Panel 3: Therapeutic Therapy: Innovating Treatment Options

Dr. Todd Edmondson, moderator

Abby Dotson, "Caring for the Elderly: Eliminating an Annual Cap on Physical Therapy Visits"

Amber Mitchell, "The Innovation of Virtual Reality Therapy"

Dani Bryant, "When Having a Good Imagination Is Bad: Body Dysmorphia and Eating Disorders"

Panel 4: New Mediums and New Messages: Imagining the Future of Art and Technology

Dr. Daniel Silliman, moderator

Taylor Williams, "Cinema Sans Sin: Imaginatively Transforming Evangelical Cinema"

Andrew Utterback, "Reimagining YouTube"

Sarah Greer, "Simulating Life: Reimagining Realism in the Art of Animation"

Panel 5: A Poverty of Imagination: Rethinking Learning and Literacy in and out of the Classroom

Mary Jackson, moderator

Ethan Wymer, "Reading into the Public Education Standards: Reimagining Learning for Elementary Students"

Lydia Helton, "Heroes and Princesses: How Imagination Can Address Poverty"

Emily Harper, "Playtime Should Not Be Over: The Importance of Play in Elementary Classrooms"

APPENDIX 9

Conference Response Sheet

Your Name: _____ Professor's Name: _____

Panel Name and Presenters: _____

For each presentation, fill in the title and take notes on the back. Turn in your sheet to the appropriate professor's collection box after the exam.

Presentation 1 Title: _____

What is your response to this argument?

Craft one insightful question to ask the presenter:

Presentation 2 Title: _____

What is your response to this argument?

Craft one insightful question to ask the presenter:

Presentation 3 Title: _____

What is your response to this argument?

Craft one insightful question to ask the presenter:

Final Response: In the space below, write one insightful question that responds to all arguments presented or write a comment that you would like to make in response to the three presentations.

Conference Evaluation Question: What was the most valuable part of the conference experience?

APPENDIX 10

Ongoing Research Assignment

Identify an area of interest or study that you would like to pursue as you move forward in your chosen field of study.

Generate the first 3 sections of a research proposal:

- Section I: Introduction/Purpose
- Section II: Research Question
- Section III: Research Strategy
- Section IV: Identify an undergraduate conference at which you could showcase your research and a potential project mentor on campus
  - ▸ Include the date and location of the conference
  - ▸ Identify submission deadlines and materials required
  - ▸ Identify a project mentor and briefly defend that choice
- Section V: Write an abstract for your project
  - ▸ Situate your project in conversation
  - ▸ Length may vary: 100–250 words

Bibliography

Askvik, Eva Ose, F. R. van der Weel, and Audrey van der Meer. "The Importance of Cursive Handwriting over Typewriting for Learning in the Classroom: A High-Density EEG Study of 12-Year-Old Children and Young Adults." *Frontiers in Psychology* 11 (July 28, 2020), https://doi.org/10.3389/fpsyg.2020.01810.

Atwood, Margaret. *Oryx and Crake.* New York: Anchor Books, 2003.

Berry, Wendell. *Standing by Words: Essays.* Berkeley: Counterpoint, 1983.

Chittister, Joan. *Wisdom Distilled from the Daily.* San Francisco: HarperCollins, 1991.

Coursen, Richard. "The Ghost of Christmas Past: Stopping by Woods on a Snowy Evening." *College English* 24, no. 12 (December 1962): 236–38.

Dillard, Annie. *The Writing Life.* New York: Harper Perennial, 1989.

Eliot, T. S. "The Love Song of J. Alfred Prufrock." In *The Wasteland and Other Writings.* New York: Modern Library, 2002.

Emerson, Ralph Waldo. "Self-Reliance." In *Emerson: The Major Prose,* edited by Ronald A. Bosco and Joel Myerson. Cambridge, MA: Belknap, 2015.

Foucault, Michel. *Politics, Philosophy, Culture: Interviews and Other Writings, 1977–1984.* Edited by Lawrence D. Kritzman. New York: Routledge, 1990.

Freire, Paolo. *Pedagogy of the Oppressed.* New York: Bloomsbury Academic, 2018.

Gadamer, H. G. *Truth and Method.* Translated by Joel Weinsheimer and Donald G. Marshall. London: Bloomsbury, 1975.

Gilbert, Elizabeth. *Big Magic: Creative Living beyond Fear.* New York: Penguin, 2016.

Grafton, Anthony. "The Death of the Footnote (Report on an Exaggera-
tion)." *Wilson Quarterly* 21, no. 1 (Winter 1997): 72–77.

Gyasi, Yaa. *Transcendent Kingdom*. New York: Vintage, 2021.

Hanh, Thich Nhat. *The Art of Communicating*. New York: HarperOne,
2013.

Hayhoe, Katharine. *Saving Us: A Climate Scientist's Case for Hope and Healing
in a Divided World*. New York: One Signal, 2021.

Heidegger, Martin. *Early Greek Thinking*. Translated by David Farrell Krell
and Frank A. Capuzzi. New York: Harper & Row, 1975.

Hirshfield, Jane. *Ten Windows: How Great Poems Transform the World*. New
York: Knopf, 2015.

hooks, bell. *Teaching Community: A Pedagogy of Hope*. New York: Routledge, 2003.

Howe, Marie. "Singularity." 2019. https://poets.org/poem/singularity.

Klinkenborg, Verlyn. *Several Short Sentences about Writing*. New York: Vintage, 2012.

Krumrei-Mancuso, E. J., and S. V. Rouse. "The Development and Validation
of the Comprehensive Intellectual Humility Scale." *Journal of Personality
Assessment* 98 (2016): 209–21.

Lamott, Anne. *Bird by Bird: Some Instructions on Writing and Life*. New York:
Anchor Books, 1994.

Leonardo, Nixaly. *Active Listening Techniques: 30 Practical Tools to Hone Your
Communication Skills*. Emeryville, CA: Rockridge, 2020.

Leroy, Sophie. "Why Is It So Hard to Do My Work? The Challenge of Attention Residue When Switching Tasks." *Organizational Behavior and
Human Decision Processes* 109, no. 2 (July 2009): 168–81.

Levertov, Denise. "Some Notes on Organic Form." *Poetry* 106, no. 6 (Sep-
tember 1965): 420–25.

Marshall, Ellen Ott. *Introduction to Christian Ethics: Conflict, Faith, and
Human Life*. Louisville: Westminster John Knox, 2018.

McCarthy, Cormac. *The Road*. New York: Vintage, 2006.

McEntyre, Marilyn Chandler. *Caring for Words in a Culture of Lies*. Grand
Rapids: Eerdmans, 2009.

———. *Word Tastings: An Essay Anthology*. Santa Barbara, CA: Santa Barbara
Review, 1998.

Miller, Stephen. *Conversation: A History of a Declining Art*. New Haven: Yale
University Press, 2006.

Monteiro, George. "Suicide and the New England Conscience: Notes on
Edith Wharton, Robinson, and Frost." *American Literary Realism* 50, no.
2 (Winter 2018): 145–51.

Oliver, Mary. "Sometimes." In *Red Bird*. Boston: Beacon, 2008.

———. "Upstream." In *Upstream: Selected Essays*. New York: Penguin, 2016.

Orwell, George. "Politics and the English Language." In *The Orwell Reader: Fiction, Essays, and Reportage*. New York: Harcourt, 1984.

Pariser, Eli. *The Filter Bubble: What the Internet Is Hiding from You*. London: Penguin, 2011.

Pinker, Steven. *The Sense of Style: The Thinking Person's Guide to Writing in the 21st Century*. New York: Penguin, 2015.

Pound, Ezra. "In the Station of the Metro." In *Personae: The Shorter Poems*, revised by Lea Baechler and A. Walton Litz. New York: New Direction, 1990.

Solnit, Rebecca. *Orwell's Roses*. New York: Viking, 2021.

Thoreau, Henry David. *A Week on the Concord and Merrimack Rivers, Walden, The Maine Woods, Cape Cod*. New York: Library of America, 1985.

Tippett, Krista. *Becoming Wise*. New York: Penguin, 2016.

Tufte, Virginia. *Artful Sentences: Syntax as Style*. Cheshire, CT: Graphics, 2006.

Watterson, Bill. *Homicidal Psycho Jungle Cat*. Kansas City, MO: Andrews McMeel, 1994.

Weil, Simone. "Reflections on the Right Use of School Studies with a View to the Love of God." In *Waiting for God*. New York: Putnam's Sons, 1953.

Williams, Joseph M., and Joseph Bizup. *Style: Lessons in Clarity and Grace*. 11th ed. New York: Pearson, 2014.

Wirzba, Norman. *The Paradise of God: Renewing Religion in an Ecological Age*. Oxford: Oxford University Press, 2007.

Zeldin, Theodore. *Conversation*. Mahwah, NJ: Hidden Spring, 1998.

Index